I0541555

PRAISE FOR I ATE MY VANISHING TWIN

"Dr. Purnell has given us a healing memoir that is refreshingly unconventional. Alternatingly heart-wrenching and hilarious, this is a riveting, heart-opening story and guide that takes the reader on the wild ride that has been the author's relationship with food—and life. At the same time, she combines her skills as a highly accomplished PhD educator and gifted healing professional to provide a counterpoint of context and insights that ground the deeply personal narrative in data, a variety of health models, and healing quotes. These medical, complementary health, and spirituality offerings give the reader a wide range of perspectives and resources to explore beyond this book. As a former holistic nutrition practitioner who has worked with many clients like Laura, there's no doubt that *I Ate My Vanishing Twin* will prove validating, inspiring, and educational for anyone who has struggled with disordered eating and is open to inner explorations and outside-the-box opportunities for wellbeing.

- Catherine Varchaver, MAT, CHHC
Former owner, Body and Soul Nutrition

I ATE MY VANISHING TWIN

TRAUMA, SPIRITUALITY, AND HUNGER:
MAKING PEACE WITH FOOD

LAURA PURNELL, PHD, ACHT

I Ate My Vanishing Twin
Trauma, Spirituality, and Hunger: Making Peace with Food

Published by Educational Alchemist, LLC
Willoughby Hills, Ohio

Copyright © 2025 by Laura Purnell

All rights reserved. No part of this publication may be reproduced, stored in a retrieval system, or transmitted in any form or by any means, electronic, mechanical, recorded, photocopied, graphic, or otherwise, without written permission of the author.

ISBNs:
Print: 979-8-9925587-0-8
Ebook: 979-8-9925587-1-5

Library of Congress Control Number: 2025927726

Subjects:
SEL014000   **SELF-HELP** / Eating Disorders & Body Image
SEL021000   **SELF-HELP** / Motivational & Inspirational
SEL031000   **SELF-HELP** / Personal Growth / General

STOP the DIET RIOT! is a trademark of Educational Alchemist.

Printed in the United States

 Formatted with Vellum

A NOTE OF CAUTION

My memoir sheds light on several emotional topics, including sexual abuse, emotional abuse, racism, and trauma. Too often, many of us can't find safe spaces and appropriate resources that enable us to explore how our experiences around these critical issues, and others as well, impact our wellbeing. If reading my story triggers overwhelm or other strong emotions, I encourage you to seek support.

RESOURCES

Call or text 988
for help if you're experiencing a mental health crisis.

National Eating Disorders Association
https://www.nationaleatingdisorders.org/

National Association of Anorexia Nervosa and Associated Disorders
1 (888)-375-7767
https://anad.org/get-help/eating-disorders-helpline/

The Rape, Abuse, and Incest National Network
1-800-656-4673

RAINN organizes the national sexual assault telephone hotline. The hotline is a referral service that can put you in contact with your local rape crisis center. You can call the hotline or access RAINN's online chat service.

With love to my daughters, Jen and Ali, and granddaughter Quinn

2024

"*After nourishment, shelter, and companionship, stories are the thing we need most in the world.*"
–Philip Pullman

"*The purpose of a storyteller is not to tell you how to think, but to give you questions to think upon.*"
-Brandon Sanderson

"*By offering up their life stories for scrutiny, these women were hoping to find some clues, some answers, to the origin of this mysterious obsession (with food, dieting, body image) that consumed their lives.*"
-Anita Johnston

I AM these women.
My gift is my story.

Vanishing Twin Syndrome (VTS) is a condition where one of the fetuses in a multiple pregnancy stops developing and is absorbed by the other fetus, the placenta, or the mother's body.

PROLOGUE

There's a diet riot going on in my head. It's got to stop!

My Quest: Finding peace with food. Befriending my hunger. Liberation from suffering.

Shining my light in the world!

This is a memoir of a healing journey.

A very thoughtful editor friend read the draft of my story and shared valuable feedback that helped shape the way the book unfolded. She also challenged me to the core, hit a nerve spot on, and helped me to see that something was missing even as it was right there in front of me. Aware that my quest is focused on stopping the diet riot in my head and making peace with food and hunger, this observant friend wrote:

"... when it comes down to it, the book fascinatingly doesn't draw a detailed picture of what your actual food experiences look/looked like. Perhaps that's because it's too painful to write about? Or because your suffering has really been about the underlying issues that contributed to the disordered relationship with eating and hunger, or ..."

I want ice cream now. My body feels shaky. I feel shame. I've got to get out of here. She's right. I feel so vulnerable. I can't write about this.

I thanked my body and brain for this heart wisdom. I went upstairs and changed the sheets, started a load of laundry, sat quietly, and let the urge to run out for ice cream pass. I stayed with feelings of shame and let them move through me. With compassion and curiosity, I gave myself some time and space to wonder why I feel embarrassed to write about my food experiences.

"Shame is the intensely painful feeling or experience of believing that we are flawed and therefore unworthy of love, belonging, and connection."
-Brené Brown

Participating in a shame exercise was one of the most healing moments I've ever experienced. During my hypnotherapy training, our cohort was invited to take turns sitting in front of the group and responding to the prompt, "Something I wouldn't want you to know about me ..." Our group had already developed trust, connections, and safety. We call this building a safe container (space) for healing. The act of sharing parts of my history that I'm ashamed of, treating the shock that came up during my sharing, being held in unconditional love, and holding sacred space for others during their sharing is one of the most significant events in my healing journey. As I write this, I'm ready to dig even deeper, to go inward, and shed light on my food experiences. Awareness matters.

So, deep breath, here goes. These are some things I wouldn't want you to know about my food experiences.

I packed ready-made toast with peanut butter to take on a cross-country trip to ensure that I'd have something to eat after dinner with others. At other times, Zone Bars, Luna Bars, Built Bars, and other bars have served as my "If I get hungry" safety net.

As a first-time Weight Watcher in college, I blended a can of asparagus into a soup I ate every day for lunch. I asked the group leader how many points were in a tablespoon of dried vegetable flakes that I added to the soup. In high school, I invented a "healthy" version of French Onion Soup. It was made of a beef bouillon cube, mozzarella cheese, and bacon bits. There were times when this was my only meal of the day.

I always took the biggest dessert and sought the one with the most frosting. I took a three-month course that focused on intuitive eating. No food was off limits. I ate dessert every night for three months. I could not imagine a day without dessert. I gained eighteen pounds.

In sixth grade, I realized that eating a filet of fish sandwich, fries, and a vanilla shake still left me feeling hungry.

In my family, it was okay to take a whole row of Oreo cookies at a time. Candy was hidden in my dad's sock drawer, and we helped ourselves. My mom's Halloween ghost cookies were famous. Cheryl's ™ cookies are the only ones that come close in taste. At one point within the last several years, I gave myself permission to eat two of those expensive cookies every night after dinner.

During my first marriage, I started throwing away food wrappers in public garbage cans so my husband and others wouldn't know what I was really eating.

I've been searching for licorice ice cream for decades. I found it in Copenhagen. Passing an ice cream stand is enough to trigger an urge to stop.

Portion control goes out the window with foods like pizza, cookies, and most chocolate. I try to control my food intake by dieting, counting calories, and labeling foods as good or bad. This never works.

In college, I saw some girls eating and purging. I watched as other girls quit eating altogether. I bought junk food in the vending machine. I started smoking.

I eat when I'm excited, lonely, angry, bored, anxious. I don't always eat when I'm hungry. I'm sometimes ashamed of my hunger.

I'm attracted to pretty, tasty things. As a curious child, I took a swig from the bottle of vanilla extract, thinking it would taste as good as it smelled. I also drank from the small bottle of green food coloring. Green is my favorite color.

My cravings soared following my hysterectomy at age forty-five. I considered driving miles for a piece of cheesecake. I could not get thoughts about food out of my mind. I discovered fancy, sweet, expensive coffee drinks.

I have been ashamed of my dysfunctional relationship with food. I'm aware that shame and fear contribute to the diet riot in my head. A part of me wondered if I would keep this chapter in my book. I could tolerate the vulnerability I feel in sharing about my nervous system breakdown (stay tuned) and the other stories that follow, yet this sharing feels exceptionally painful.

I grieve the amount of time and energy I've expended on engaging in power struggles with my thoughts over food, weight, body image, self-worth—all of it. Researchers at the Institute of HeartMath™ write, "It's our heart coherence that makes it easier to sustain emotional commitment, reduce stress, and create healthier eating habits."[1]

A person is clearly out of coherence (the alignment of the heart, brain, and hormones) when they are walking around with a diet riot in their head. I find the deluge of messaging about nutrition and diets that spills forth from social media, friends and family, the medical and pharmaceutical communities, and the food industry overwhelming. Food companies in the United States spend almost $14 billion per year on advertising![2] Intrusive thoughts about food and eating seem to have a life of their own.

> *"Shame corrodes the very part of us that believes we are capable of change."*
> -Brené Brown

To continue sharing my experiences related to food and hunger, I invite you to witness what goes on in my head.

Throughout my day, I often experience intrusive thoughts about food, eating, body image, and weight. These are persistent and unwanted thoughts that can be hard to banish. They can be as fleeting as *don't look in the mirror*, or a bit more complex. *At 1500 calories a day for thirty-five weeks, I should be able to weigh x by Christmas.* I frequently experience an obsessive focus on calories, meal planning, dieting, and avoiding certain foods. These thoughts are often all-or-nothing.

*I will only do Keto for three weeks, which means I need to shop for
more protein and throw out the frozen meals.*

The most painful food thoughts come from my inner critic. Negative
self-talk about food choices and body image run on automatic pilot.
I've made a great deal of progress managing and eliminating many of
these self-defeating thoughts. Here's a taste of what the diet riot
sounds like.

> I'm so overwhelmed that I can't even make a grocery
> list. This is craziness. I better change my goal for
> macronutrients.
> No butter's allowed on that baked potato.
> Are they judging me for eating pancakes?
> I'll lose ten pounds this month.
> I feel great! I've lost a pound.
> I'm tired of eating the same meals all week.
> I can never have ice cream again.
> Steak is bad for me. I want a steak.
> It's scary to eat out.
> I look fat in that picture.
> I don't trust myself around food.
> Just order a pizza.
> I can't give up coffee and diet Coke.
> I want cake now!
> What if I'm still hungry?
> I WILL NOT stop at that bakery.
> I'll start over on Monday.

Several themes run through my intrusive thoughts. It's clear that my
preoccupation with food, constantly thinking about what to eat next,
calorie counting, or meal planning sucks vital life force energy out of
my being. My fear of hunger causes anxiety about getting hungry and

not having food available, which has led to overeating and eating in private. Obsessing about my body weight, appearance, and the impact of food on my physical appearance obscures the reality that I am a worthy, divine, spiritual being in a human body.

I acknowledge that I've experienced shame for feeling hungry. I didn't set boundaries when people made comments about my food choices. I didn't push back when other people attempted to control my food intake, influence my weight, or commented on my weight gain or loss. I took on others' shame around eating as my own. I know that I also judge people who carry extra weight.

When friends and family crossed personal boundaries (because I didn't have any for a long time) about food, hunger, eating, and body image and made attempts to manage me, their comments often sounded like this:

> *"You're not going to eat that are you?"*
> *"You must be too full to have dessert."*
> *"You ate breakfast. How can you be hungry for lunch?"*
> *"This portion is so big I bet none of us will eat it all."*
> *"I can go all day without eating. How can you be hungry?"*
> *"I'm afraid you'll get fat."*
> *"How much do you weigh?"*
> *"You look great. Are you losing weight?"*
> *"You can't have that."*
> *"She'll have the salad."*
> *"I thought you were on a diet."*
> *"You won't get a new job at your size."*
> *"That food is not good for you."*
> *"I can't believe you ate the whole thing!" (I can't believe I ate the whole thing.)*

And there's the passive-aggressive, non-verbal look of "shame on you."

I'm aware that I have a choice to accept or reject shaming words, actions, intentions, and energy that others project on me. I'm also human and have layers upon layers of shame that continue to surface so that I can heal. Shaming people about their food choices and hunger—or anything—inevitably has significant negative effects on their mental and physical health. I am walking proof.

Shaming can lead to heightened levels of stress, anxiety, and depression, making individuals feel unworthy and isolated. Criticism and judgment can erode a person's self-esteem, leading to a negative self-image. Shaming is also a common trigger for emotional eating, where individuals eat to cope with their feelings rather than out of physical hunger.[3] As painful as this is to write and acknowledge, I know that this is true for me.

People who have experienced shame about food, hunger, and body image often develop behaviors that don't serve them. People may start eating in secret to avoid judgment, which can lead to unhealthy eating patterns and further isolation. Shame can also exacerbate disordered eating behaviors, such as binge eating, restrictive eating, or purging, to cope with emotional pain. Shaming reinforces societal stigmas around body size and food choices, perpetuating harmful stereotypes and discrimination. Have you read a personal ad recently? I have. Not-so-subtle screening looks like this: "Seeking a woman who takes care of herself; is in good shape; has a petite shape; has included a full body picture; and is not overweight." Over time, shame has contributed to my unhealthy, disordered eating behaviors. As I continue to heal my unfounded shame, the positive impact on my wellbeing is enormous.

I chose to surface and examine traumatic events that have happened to me and in relationships with others as a means of facing challenges on my heroine's journey. Today, I approach my relationship with food and hunger with compassion and understanding.

> Personal Journal Entry
> 10/20/20
> Dear Laura,
> I long to be connected to you. I've never given up hope that you'd come to realize that I've got your back. (I know you love puns.) We have our own special ways of communicating. So much wisdom resides inside of me/us. Your emotions—energy in motion—reside in me/us. Felt sensations are a wonderful barometer of your wellbeing and balance. Please see me, feel me, know me. I am so grateful, my beloved, for the sacred role I've been given to make it possible for you to experience being a spiritual being in a physical body. I'm resilient. I'm strong. I am miraculous. I so hope that you can grow to trust me. I am divinely created; vitality and balance are my natural states. I am a/your healer. I am part of your sense of self. I'd love more compassion, more patience, more love.
> Much love,
> Your body

Personal Soul Collage Card: Visualizing Compassion, Peace, & Love

REFLECTIONS

I moved into my house several weeks before the world shut down in response to COVID-19. As soon as we were able to leave home and address necessary business, I went to my local garden center to buy two big plants. In my opinion, having life-giving plants in one's home qualifies as essential business. I could tell that one plant was going to bloom at some point. I waited. Nothing happened. I waited, and I waited. One day, my plant blossomed. It grew a spathe—a white, hoodlike structure that encloses the flower cluster. My new plant is a peace plant, also known as a peace lily. Peace lilies are valued for their elegant appearance and ability to purify the air.

As I sat in appreciation of my pretty plant, a thought struck me. My plant was taking time for rest and recovery, growth and development, and bud formation. Are there spaces in my life where I simply need to give peace a chance?

My story is about making peace with food and hunger. In the end, I recognize it's about my quest to live authentically, with feelings of peace flowing from my awareness that I am a divine, spiritual, multi-dimensional being. To experience and sustain this knowing, I need to grow and develop. I need to dig deeper and explore the roots of my obsessions and compulsions around food and hunger. As I've continued to dig, it's become increasingly clear to me that I'm ready to heal deeply held levels of shame.

I aspire to teach and write like Brené Brown. She defines shame as "the intensely painful feeling or experience of believing that we are flawed and therefore unworthy of love and belonging."[3] No wonder this section has been so hard to write. Brown's Shame Resilience Theory outlines four strategies to build resilience against shame: recognizing shame triggers, practicing critical awareness, reaching out, and speaking shame.[4]

We must learn to recognize physically when we are in the grip of shame so that we can name it and find our way through it. I recognized shame moving through me when I read my editor friend's insights about the elephant in the room. I felt shame about articulating my experiences with food. I wondered if I was really ready to go public with this. I connected in a very deep, somatic (in my body) way with my faulty belief that I am flawed and, therefore, unworthy. Ouch. At the same time, I understand that my soul presented this opportunity for me to change my negative beliefs. I am divinely perfect. I am worthy of love, acceptance, and belonging!

I'm developing critical awareness about the unrealistic and unattainable expectations that I have for myself (and are projected by others) that trigger feelings of shame around my dysfunctional relationship with food and eating. I'm much more conscious that healing shame is a key step on my path to experiencing peace with food and hunger.

Writing and sharing my heroine's journey is my way of reaching out, connecting, and owning my story. Throughout this process, I've developed greater empathy for myself and for others who have experienced similar struggles. At our core, all humans need to feel safe and connected.

So, I am speaking my shame. Experiencing judgment and keeping secret my fears and unconscious feelings of unworthiness have contributed to my unhealthy relationship with food and hunger. Writing my memoir gives me the opportunity to speak and heal my shame, reclaim my vital life-force energy, and live authentically. I feel lighter.

> "If you put shame in a Petri dish, it needs three things to grow exponentially: secrecy, silence, and judgment. If you put the same amount of shame in a Petri dish and douse it with empathy, it can't survive."
> -Brené Brown

NOTES

1. Doc Childre and Deborah Rozman. *Stopping Emotional Eating:* HeartMath™ Stress and Weight Management Program. (Waterfront Digital Press. 2017) 27-53.

2. University of Connecticut Rudd Center for Food Policy, "Food Marketing." November 2024. https://uconnruddcenter.org/research/food-marketing/?form=MG0AV3.

3. M. Wong and M. Quian. "The Role of Shame in Emotional Eating." 2016. https://psycnet.apa.org/record/2016-58844-009?form=MG0AV3https:%2F%2Fpositivepsychology.com%2Fshame-resilience-theory%2F

4. Jeremy Sutton, PhD. "Shame Resilience Theory: Advice from Brené Brown." June 14, 2017. https://positivepsychology.com/shame-resilience-theory/.

LET'S DO THIS!

~~last ever~~

My ~~most recent~~ ^ most recent binge was on ~~Christmas day, June 13, 2023~~, in 2024. How do I start sharing my story of recovery when I'm still learning how to transform stress, manage emotional reactions, change my emotional behavior, and create a new neural habit? Granted, I've made *lots* of progress in the past decades. The most important nugget in this book might well be this: It's okay. Write it anyway. Live life now. This is my dream. Let go and let the story unfold. I AM divinely perfect, right now, as is. So are you!

My soul was so excited about my purpose and passion that I simply couldn't wait to get here. I was born two months early, on May 14, 1956, weighing in at three pounds, fourteen ounces with a full head of hair. The truth is, I was born into this world whole. I forgot that I came in shining.

I forgot. And so did you.

Perinatal is a term used to describe the time, usually a few weeks, immediately before and after birth. According to Annie Brook, during this developmental, preverbal, yet ever so conscious sacred time, human souls enter the world with three basic questions about their existence. *"Is the world safe? Will I survive? Will I survive in relationship?"*[1]

Recovery from disordered eating is possible when we journey through the process of **rediscovering** who we truly are. Perhaps we should say that we are **rediscovering** rather than recovering! We are divinely perfect. We are light. We came here to remember our true essence. In planning for this lifetime, we chose our parents, siblings, partners, challenges, and so much more. Before we forgot our true essence, we planned a life that would offer opportunities for spiritual growth. **So, recovery from disordered eating and every other life challenge is really a spiritual path.** Since we are spiritual beings in human bodies, recovery from disordered eating is also a neurobiological healing journey.

Key points for the journey of rediscovering:

- There is nothing wrong with you, me, us.
- Disordered eating is a trauma response.
- Unconsciously, this behavior helped us survive.
- When we heal our bodies and nurture our souls, we make peace with food, hunger, and our bodies.

This is not a diet book, but it will help those struggling with overeating. This is not a religious book, but it will help those seeking greater consciousness and spiritual growth. This is not a scientific document, but it will encourage readers to wonder. This is not a resource full of quick fixes for people in pain or for people trying to fix others.

My story is about what marvelous, multi-faceted human beings we are. It's about learning to access the untapped power of the heart. It's a shout-out to the world about the magnificence of the mind-body-spirit connection. This is a testament to our ability to heal.

It's about the values of the heart: love, care, appreciation, compassion, forgiveness, non-judgment. This is not a substitute for therapy. This little memoir is my story of waking up, owning up, and growing up. In doing so, I have the energy and grace to follow my passion to teach and help people heal. It's an invitation for you to move mountains as well.

This is the story of my personal heroine's journey to answer the questions: Why do I do what I do (stress/emotional eating)? ~~How do I fix this?~~ What can I learn from this pattern of behavior that no longer serves me? How do I heal now that I've **rediscovered** my true, divine essence and my purpose in life? How do I heal now that I know **it's not my fault**?

I invite you to settle in for a fascinating, often far-out, hopefully compelling, vulnerable, funny, sometimes disturbing, going to push boundaries by talking about things good girls (and boys) don't talk about memoir. This, my friends, is the story of my healing journey. **My heroine's journey!** It's told from my perspective. The souls who have crossed my path along the way may have perceived events differently. That's okay. My intention is to tell the truth, as I know it now, from my heart, in hopes that others will connect with my story. I believe that heart-centered connections manifest healing.

I thought it was about the weight
I dug deeper
I thought it was about betrayal
I dug deeper
I thought it was about the shame
I dug deeper
I thought it was about two divorces
I dug deeper

I thought it was about the stress
Autoimmune condition
Job
Whistleblowing
PhD
Nervous breakdown
Single parenting
Emotional abuse
Sexual abuse
Thyroid condition
Lichen Sclerosis
Adults who bullied
Kids who bullied
Pneumonia
Tonsillectomy
Premature birth and the incubator
Disorganized attachment style
Abandonment
I kept digging and went back to the source
To the source of the pain
The needs not met
That caused the shock
A result of the trauma
That manifested the beliefs that
I'm not safe
I might die
There is never enough
It's my fault
I AM HUNGRY
There is something wrong with me
I ate my vanishing twin!

And to ease the pain, I
Pleased others so they wouldn't leave me

Suppressed my needs and wants to the point that I didn't think I
had any
Became an exceptionally good girl
Smoked cigarettes
Grew into a perfectionist
Often procrastinated
Became obsessed with dieting and restricting food
Avoided painful emotions
Developed a Pollyanna worldview
Stayed in painful, dysfunctional relationships for too long
Didn't rock the boat
Looked like I've got it all together
Didn't trust
Became an overachieving workaholic
Restricted food and skipped meals
Became afraid of food and hunger
Binged on food, TV, shopping, intellectualizing, and work in my
efforts to avoid feeling

Shame,
Powerlessness,
And anxiety.

Like an archeologist, I dug, and I dug, and I just kept digging in hopes of discovering the antidote for my suffering around food, hunger, and body image. This anguish presents itself as a diet riot in my head, a crack in my heart, and a split in my soul.

WHAT'S WRONG WITH ME?

Oprah Winfrey and Dr. Bruce Perry propose that we no longer ask, "What's wrong with you?" instead, the fundamental question should be, "What happened to you?" [2] Canadian Physician and author Gabor Maté believes that what happened to you is called a traumatic event. He explains that trauma is what happens *inside* you because of what happened to you. Many experts agree that dysfunctional eating and other addictions can all be traced to childhood trauma. [3]

Maté often talks about how trauma can lead to a disconnection from emotions, difficulty staying in the present moment, and negative views of oneself, others, and the world.[4] But this doesn't sound or look like me. Does it?

I'm done digging—at least for now. I'm ready to examine and reflect on what's happened *inside* of me because of trauma. The treasures and clues I've found so far in my quest to make peace with food and hunger include memories, pictures, stories, lots and lots of books, podcasts, training, and alternative healing modalities.

So begins my heroine's journey inside myself to explore traumatic events that happened to me, causing physical, chemical, emotional, and spiritual stress, knocking my body out of balance, resulting in behaviors that unconsciously helped me regulate my nervous system, which now cause me pain. Are some of my thoughts and behaviors originally rooted in my drive to survive contributing to the suffering I've experienced in my relationship with food and hunger? And if so, what am I supposed to do? How am I supposed to be?

As we begin this journey together, I borrow from the words of author and trauma therapist C.J. Llewelyn. Her hopes echo mine.

"This book is for anyone who wants to stop running from their suffering, which presents in the body (all of us) and start gathering information on how to heal themselves."
-C.J. Llewelyn [5]

"The biggest takeaway I would like for you to get from this book is to embrace the idea that your body holds over three-quarters of what you need to know about yourself in order to heal old wounds."
-C.J. Llewelyn [6]

NOTES

1. Annie Brook. *Birth's Hidden Legacy: Volume 1* (*How Surprising Beliefs from Infancy Limit Successful Child and Adult Behavior*). (Smart Body Books, 2014), 41.

2. Bruce Perry and Oprah Winfrey. *What Happened to You? Conversations on Trauma, Resilience and Healing.* (New York: Flat Iron Books, 2021.)

3. Gabor Maté. "How Childhood Trauma Leads to Addiction." YouTube, January 19,

2021. https://youtu.be/BVg2bfqblGI?si=PTFzS-LMNXaVibO9

4. Maté. "How Childhood Trauma Leads to Addiction."

5. C.J. Llewelyn, M.Ed. *Chakras and the Vagus Nerve: Tap Into the Healing Combination of Subtle Energy & Your Nervous System.* (Woodbury, MN: Llewelyn Publications, 2023.) 1.

6. Llewelyn, *Chakras and the Vagus Nerve*, 5.

SECTION ONE
MY HEROINE'S JOURNEY

CHAPTER 1
THE PROTAGONIST

Since I'm the main character in my story, it's important that you get to know a little bit about me. I play the leading role, known as the protagonist. This is where I give you a glimpse of me, the heroine, living my ordinary life. I'm a mom, grandmother, mother-in-law, sister, aunt, friend, teacher, healer, and seeker.

I was so excited to arrive in this world that I was born two months prematurely, weighed three pounds fourteen ounces, and spent a few months in an incubator. My maternal grandmother, who lived with us and helped care for us, died when I was five. I had my tonsils removed at age six. I was the social yet "sick child," having frequent earaches, strep throat, and pneumonia. I was an inquisitive child, taking a bite out of a frozen handrail and having my lips and face gently removed by the pediatrician. And a few years later, I crashed face-first into a tree while riding my bike. I have chipped teeth and great full lips. I was teased mercilessly.

A friend of the family sexually molested me at age eleven and I didn't tell a soul. My thought form became *it just happened once. It wasn't rape.* I married at twenty-four, stayed in this emotionally stressful relationship for six years, and brought two beautiful daughters into this world. I divorced at thirty, taking my newborn and three-year-old to live with my parents and then on our own. I felt free, exhilarated, energetic, focused, worried, anxious, and angry. I buried the negative feelings and continued as a successful, competent, professional, and happy woman as my daughters grew up.

My dad died when I was thirty-six. I had a nervous breakdown at forty and was diagnosed with anxiety and depression.

I co-founded a public charter school. I left shortly after it opened. I was excited, motivated, proud, worried, anxious, angry, rageful, disappointed, embarrassed, and grief-stricken. I buried the negative feelings and continued as a successful, competent, professional, and happy woman. I left behind what I thought was the manifestation of my purpose and passion in this world.

I married again. I finished my dissertation and presented a paper in Durban, South Africa, shortly after 9/11. This experience changed my life. I was happy, adventurous, grateful, worried, anxious, angry, resentful, and ashamed. I buried these negative feelings and continued as a successful, competent, professional, and happy woman. I got a promotion and moved to a new city.

I experienced what I perceived to be the biggest and most significant trauma of my life. My actions significantly contributed to my boss being fired. I was thrilled, excited, motivated, courageous, worried, anxious, fearful, rageful, angry, sad, grief-stricken, and lonely. I buried the negative feelings and continued as a courageous, almost renegade hero. I took a demotion, paid thousands of dollars in legal fees, and left town.

I separated and later divorced. I was worried, anxious, ashamed, and angry. I buried the negative feelings and continued as an increasingly successful, competent, professional, and happy woman. I moved home to care for my mom, who was diagnosed with dementia and

Alzheimer's. This experience helped me heal old wounds. My mom died when I was fifty-five, six weeks before my oldest daughter's wedding.

Between 2007-2013, I worked as a superintendent in a large urban school district. I loved this city and work. I remain passionate about and oriented toward action that will make schools equitable, meaningful, and safe places for all. I retired early and started my own business.

I trained in hypnotherapy, breathwork, Reiki, metaphysics, and energy psychology. I began seeing clients and studying in a mystery school.

I am increasingly aware of the impact of trauma and shock on children, families, and adults who serve in school districts. I've learned to recognize when my body is experiencing shock. I was diagnosed with complex post-traumatic stress disorder.

I completed a sprint triathlon with my daughter. COVID-19 happened. I moved. I underwent two ear surgeries. I spent three days in the hospital with COVID-19. I experienced isolation, along with the rest of the world.

My family has grown in wonderful ways. My two sons-in-law and four grandchildren, along with my two adult daughters, are the loves of my life. I went on my first date in more than twenty years. I've been on every diet on the planet.

Light and Dark

At this stage in my life, I'm aware of my strengths and unique gifts. As part of an interactive heroine's Journey, [1] I connected with many of my strengths—resources that have served me well along my healing journey. As you read my list, I hope some will resonate as your gifts as well!

Laura's strengths: empathy, compassion, perseverance, faith, curiosity, perspective, emotional intelligence, creativity, leadership, humility, exuberance, self-discipline, connection, appreciation of beauty and excellence, humor, intelligence, bravery, optimism, determination, service, friendship, imagination, spirituality, judgment, closeness, self-awareness, social justice, inspiration, mercy, intimacy, and enthusiasm

Shadow work

I've engaged in shadow work as part of my healing and spiritual journey. Learning to navigate my levels of consciousness and integrate healed and wounded parts of myself is helping me live a more balanced and authentic life. Befriending my shadow self has helped.

We all have a shadow self. The archetypal shadow self refers to aspects of us that exist beyond conscious awareness. According to the founders of The Wellness Institute, the shadow is made up of repressed emotions, hidden fears, weaknesses, and traits that we find unacceptable or unlikable.[2] To experience and shine light in the world, it's important that we recognize and integrate the darker parts of ourselves. Integrating your shadow self is a profound journey of self-discovery and self-acceptance. By acknowledging and embracing these hidden aspects, we can achieve a more holistic and authentic understanding of who we are. As you look at my list, you may begin to wonder, with compassion, if you share some of these parts. Awareness is how integration begins.

Laura's Shadow Self: perfectionist, people pleaser, judge, know-it-all, procrastinator, anger, fear, insecure, control freak, workaholic, naive, egotistical, lazy

In getting to know me, the protagonist, I hope you'll get a sense of my head, my heart, and my spirit as you continue this journey with me.

Acrylic Self Portrait: Unbridled Grace

NOTES

1. John Drimmer. "Heros Journey® Interactive." 2013. https://herosjourneyinteractive.com/.
2. Diane Zimberoff and David Hartman, David. *Overcoming Shock: Healing the Traumatized Mind and Heart.* (Corner, NJ: New Horizon Press, 2014) 257.

CHAPTER 2

CALL TO EMBARK ON A JOURNEY OF TRANSFORMATION

T've framed my story as a simplified version of Joseph Campbell's hero's journey.[1] An article published in *Scientific American* asserts that people who frame their own life as a hero's journey find more significance in it. "When people start to see their own lives as heroic quests, we discovered, they report less depression and can cope better with challenges."[2]

This call had been stirring subtly inside me for a long time. It ebbed and flowed. The call to adventure, no matter the risk, didn't happen in a day. The quest to blossom came from the depths of my soul. **The tension between my insides (knowing that I am divine and perfect as is) and my outsides (eating-related behaviors that manifested as disturbances to living my whole, authentic life) became unbearable.**

"Humans are a walking contradiction. We are at once pure essence from a higher realm and gritty animal that strives to keep the species going. No wonder our human race gets so easily distracted and confused." [3]

-C.J. Llewelyn

The realization that disordered eating, and all addictions for that matter, can be traced to childhood trauma, and my experience of taking on the belief that I ate my vanishing twin prompted me to act, to set out on my journey of transformation.

"And the day came when the risk to remain tight in a bud was more painful than the risk it took to blossom." [4]
-Anais Nin

This quote has been meaningful to me for an exceptionally long time. In my early forties, I got a butterfly tattooed on my inner calf. This has served as a visual reminder that everything I need to blossom exists inside of me. The phrase highlights the idea that there comes a point when staying within one's comfort zone or hiding away from the world becomes more unbearable than the unknown risks associated with acting and seeking personal growth. It emphasizes the importance of welcoming change and taking chances. Now, the potential for transformation and fulfillment far outweighs the possible pain and uncertainty of stepping into the unknown. The process of authoring my story has helped me to clarify the challenges I'm exploring and the purpose of my quest.

As I set out on my adventure, I'm wondering what spiritual lessons am I to learn from my compulsive behaviors around food, hunger, eating, and body image. How do I heal so that I can live my life fully, authentically, peacefully? What am I to create that will help others heal and raise their consciousness?

I was taught that connecting with one's higher self (God, Spirit, Nature, or whatever a person perceives to be the magnificent energy that manifested the universe in the first place) through meditation, prayer, or other spiritual practice, requires a combination of both effort and grace bestowed. With my metaphorical backpack full of grace, and **huge** effort, divinely guided, I set out on my journey.

REFLECTIONS

"Nothing ever goes away until it has taught us what we need to know."
-Attributed to Pema Chödrön

I used to get swept up in magical thinking. I'd pray to wake up at my ideal healthy weight and shape, liberated from all suffering associated with food, hunger, and body image. The healing would take place overnight or in front of a large audience while I was teaching. Oprah would invite me to talk about the miracle I'd just experienced. We'd all be in awe. Many would be inspired by my experience and want to follow me. I'd step up and out as the spiritual teacher I know I'm meant to be.

I do believe in miracles. I've experienced them. I believe that as our world continues to change, we'll witness many more miracles. We've already heard stories of spontaneous remission or spontaneous healing, the unexpected and unexplained recovery from a serious illness or condition without conventional medical treatment or intervention. I believe that divine healing does happen.

Part of my journey is to keep my faith in miracles while accepting and surrendering to the notion that a divine, quick, and complete healing isn't in my best interest or for my greatest good right now! In other words, I'm learning that my healing is about the journey, not the destination. I get this on an intellectual level (thinking, brain) and I'm beginning to feel this in my body (emotion, heart).

My journey itself holds profound significance and is worth sharing. It's during the quest that we experience growth, learn lessons, and make memories. The difficulties, the challenges, and the unexpected moments all shape us and add depth to our lives.

Sometimes, the destination isn't even where we thought it would be, but the journey prepares us for wherever we end up. This is a new kind of writing for me. I don't know how my story will end. When solving problems, or taking on a big project, I usually begin with the end in mind. As I write, I often ask myself what point I'm trying to get across. Am I expecting to have a hopeful answer or some wisdom to share at the end of my story? Is sharing my story enough in and of itself?

That said, let's get going!

NOTES

1. Ben Rogers, Kurt Fray, and Mike Christen. "To Lead a Meaningful Life, Become Your Own Hero." 2023. https://herosjour neyinteractive.com/.

2. Rogers, Fray, and Christen. "To Lead a Meaningful Life, Become Your Own Hero."

3. Llewelyn. *Chakras and the Vagus Nerve.* 14.

4. The Socratic Method. "Quote Meanings and Interpretations." 2024.https://www.socratic-method.com/quote-meanings-interpreta tions/anais-nin-and-the-day-came-when-the-risk-to-remain-tight-in-a-bud-was-more-painful-than-the-risk-it-took-to-blossom.

CHAPTER 3

I ATE MY VANISHING TWIN

"To be born a twinless twin is a potent birthright that spins one's life in a certain direction, like being born with a musical or mathematical genius, or growing quickly to a height of seven feet. There is a psychic pain that not only endures for life but becomes more severe as time passes. To deal with an adult twinless twin is to experience a person suffering extreme inner torment of unresolved grief." [1]
-Brent Babcock

I didn't know that I had an identical twin who vanished in the second trimester of our coming into this world together. Doctors at the Cleveland Clinic write, "After the first trimester, pregnancies involving vanishing twin syndrome are considered high-risk. High-risk pregnancies involve a greater chance that your baby will have health problems or that you'll have your baby early."[2] The phenomenon of one twin not surviving in utero is not that uncommon. It is estimated that one in eight pregnancies begin as multiples.

Some babies opt out of the birthing and earthing experience as part of their soul's journey. The story of my vanishing twin is not one that's been handed down as many birth narratives are. My mother would not have been aware that she was carrying twins, and she passed away before I could share my discovery. In the spirit of "you can't make this stuff up," here is how I came to experience and remember my twin.

As part of my training to become certified as an advanced clinical hypnotherapist, I had the opportunity to work with some of the most gifted practitioners in the country. We learned by doing. I facilitated numerous hypnotherapies, breathwork, and psychodrama sessions. I was also the client, assisting others in their own learning while healing physically, emotionally, mentally, and spiritually in ways I never dreamed possible!

Betrayal

As my healing journey unfolded, I recognized that betrayal was a pattern in my life. At this point, I understood that we attract our own experiences. Why had I been attracting experiences characterized by such disloyalty? I've been challenged by several traumatic and public betrayals in my career. I've also been married and divorced twice. In the language of hypnotherapy, I was ready to "go back to the source, back to the original source of betrayal." Hypnotherapy, in the context of a psychodrama, was my deep dive back to the source.

I found myself in a familiar place. Frozen. I was back in the womb. I was not alone. My beloved other half, my identical twin, had accompanied me only so far into this lifetime. While in a safe trance, surrounded by people I trusted, all my senses were aware that my mother miscarried a baby, my twin, at the beginning of her second trimester. I experienced a paralyzing sense of loss, grief, and betrayal.

I took on several beliefs, imprints, and preverbal knowing that my body remembers and my unconscious mind has kept buried.

> *It's my fault.*
> *She died of starvation.*
> *I'm not safe.*
> *I'm going to die.*
> *I'll always be hungry.*
> *There's never enough.*
> *I ate my vanishing twin.*

And so I unconsciously went into survival mode and adopted behaviors based on faulty beliefs about myself and my world.

I began to wonder, is this the original trauma that occurred before birth and started the imbalance that is manifesting itself in my adult life as disordered eating, depression, and anxiety? The source of betrayal that I sought to understand and heal may have been "twin loss shock, the unconscious feeling of bewildering grief at the inexplicable loss of a twin in the womb."[3] When a twin dies during pregnancy, a phenomenon known as Vanishing Twin Syndrome (VTS) occurs. The tissue from the vanishing twin is mostly reabsorbed by the mother's body and by the surviving twin.

As part of the healing process, with support from my spiritual connections and wise adult self (also known as my resources), I was guided to change faulty beliefs and conclusions that formed long before I developed spoken language.

OLD BELIEFS & BEHAVIORS	NEW BELIEFS & BEHAVIORS
I was betrayed and abandoned. I began people pleasing. I stay in unhealthy relationships for too long. I don't set clear boundaries.	Babies experience feelings, and I honor that my experience of losing my identical twin was traumatic, and that I felt abandoned. We both chose this experience so that we would grow spiritually. I am a spiritual being having a physical experience in a body. I am not my birth story. I've learned about boundaries and consistently set them.
It's my fault. I became co-dependent. I couldn't say no. I became a rescuer. I always tried to be upbeat even when I didn't feel like it. I kept quiet to avoid arguments.	It's not my fault. Her soul chose not to stay. I release guilt and shame. I feel my grief and let it go. I set healthy boundaries. I empower people. I speak my truth.
She died of starvation. I could not identify my needs. It's my fault.	There may not have been enough nourishment for the two of us. I surrender and release things that are out of my control. I'm aware of my needs and meet them. I eat when I'm hungry. It's not my fault.
I'm not safe. I don't ask for help. I'm stuck and helpless. I let people judge what and when I eat. I developed all-or-nothing beliefs.	Babies experience feelings, and I honor that my experience in the womb felt unsafe at times. I am safe now. Most of the time, I have resources and choices when I do feel unsafe. I listen to my body for cues of safety and signs that something is not right or good for me. I trust my inner knowing. I set healthy boundaries.
I'm going to die. I don't feel painful emotions. I acted powerless. I became a victim.	We're all going to die sometime, and I am not afraid of dying. I practice mindfulness and living in the present moment. I feel all my emotions and don't dwell on painful ones. I choose love, not fear. I trust my soul's plan for this lifetime. I have everything I need. I am a creator.

OLD BELIEFS & BEHAVIORS	NEW BELIEFS & BEHAVIORS
I'll always be hungry. I ate compulsively. I became afraid of hunger. I forgot my natural hunger signals. I developed all-or-nothing beliefs.	I have access to an abundance of healthy food. I eat when I'm hungry. Most of the time, I stop when I'm full. I am practicing healthy ways of balancing my nervous system. I trust my body. I surrender to the wisdom of my body.
There's never enough. I became obsessed with dieting. I looked for answers outside of myself. I became caught up in a cycle of restricting and overeating. I developed all-or-nothing attitudes.	I have what I need. I am abundantly blessed in all areas of my life. There is enough for everyone. I release attachments to earthly, material things. I am not a victim. I don't restrict food groups. I trust my inner knowing. I enjoy healthy and delicious food. I practice intuitive eating.
I ate my vanishing twin. I didn't set boundaries. I felt guilty and ashamed. I felt betrayed. I didn't recognize my grief. I was attracted to situations of betrayal so I could heal that wounded part of me.	I didn't eat my vanishing twin. Her body passed in some natural way. I release guilt and shame. I release unresolved grief. I set healthy boundaries. I love myself. I no longer attract people or situations that lead to betrayal. I'm rewriting my birth story. I'm sharing my heroine's journey as I practice and learn to STOP the DIET RIOT!

Vanishing twin syndrome is listed in the International Statistical Classification of Diseases. (651.33). [4]

Vanishing twin happens when one of a set of twin fetuses disappears from the womb, typically resulting in a normal singleton pregnancy. Brook, a pre- and peri-natal expert, describes challenges that the surviving twin may encounter.

Vanishing Twin Fears and Complications of Identity [5]

- Confusion about who stayed and who left (went back to spirit)
- Possible gender identity confusion if the opposite gender vanished
- Unexplainable grief and fear of loss of connection- sense of perpetual abandonment
- Longing to be overly connected to the spirit world (often expressed as a strong heart connection and link to the dolphin species)
- Continuous longing for that special other; seeking the "twin flame" partner
- Inability to allow intimacy with one's partner; not accepting them for fear of loss, not accepting them as "good enough," insisting they be "special"

I've come to understand how these deeply held yet hidden core beliefs and accompanying behaviors have impacted my life. I'm learning to practice compassion for self. I'm in the process of healing guilt, shame, grief, and a very primal fear of dying that have been part of the fabric of my life for more than six decades.

Let's Talk About Hypnotherapy and Breathwork

Hypnotherapy is a therapeutic practice that uses guided hypnosis to help a client reach a trance-like state of focus, concentration, diminished peripheral awareness, and heightened suggestibility. It is now promoted by the American Psychological Association as a therapy beneficial for pain, anxiety, and mood disorders, helping people change negative habits such as smoking, and for managing emotions such as fear.[5] Therapists bring about hypnosis with the help of mental imagery and soothing verbal repetition that ease the patient into a trance-like state. Clients are guided to change faulty beliefs and to identify new, healthy viewpoints and behaviors.

I began to learn more about the trauma I experienced at birth as I continued my hypnotherapy and breathwork sessions. My mind and body hold memories of being born with the umbilical cord wrapped around my neck. During sessions, I often coughed, choked, held my breath, and described my inner knowing that I was being strangled. My face turned red, and marks would become visible under my chin. To this day, when I am excited or anxious, you can see a faint, small scar on my neck. I don't like to wear clothing around my throat. Bessel van der Kolk, an expert in the field of trauma, writes that "our bodies remember and store the effects of trauma, even if our conscious minds may not fully recall the traumatic events. This means that trauma can have lasting impacts on our physical and emotional wellbeing, influencing how we respond to stress and interact with the world around us."[6]

At the beginning of my story, I mentioned that you can't make this stuff up. During a hypnotherapy session early in my training, I smelled ether being released from my body. Several of my colleagues have described smelling ether being released as clients regressed to the womb and experienced the birthing process during sessions. Although I've not found scientific evidence that drugs given to mothers during labor are passed on to the baby and remain stored in the body, this was a profound experience for me. In addition, I was certain that there were fresh flowers in the room. Others have shared that they believe the smell of fresh flowers is a sign that an angel or other divine spiritual being is present.

My breathwork teacher describes integral breath therapy as "a highly personal, experiential process that uses specific breathing techniques to clear out physical, mental, and emotional blocks or stresses. This is a safe and proven method of utilizing simple breathing practices to quickly and easily enter a non-ordinary state of consciousness. This trance state allows unconscious and previously repressed thoughts and emotions to rise to the surface for release and integration."[7]

During a series of breathwork sessions following my hypnotherapy/psychodrama, I received a vision of a fertilized egg splitting in two. My identical twin is a girl. I've come to call her Grace.

Other Birth Issues

My training and firsthand experiences confirm that birth traumas impact beliefs that we took on during the process of coming into this world and often result in relationship and individual issues that impact our wellbeing. [8,9]

For example, according to Brook, babies like me, who were born prematurely and spent their first days or weeks in an incubator, may have taken on these faulty beliefs:

I am weak
I am too small
I am frail
I can't make it
I am helpless
I'm not ready
In addition, relational and individual issues may surface over
the lifetime, including:
Fear of abandonment

Fear of intimacy
Poor time-concept
Looks to material objects for emotional warmth[10]

This Girl Walks on Fire!

One of my greatest adventures was having the opportunity to walk on fire. Twice! This experience was part of my hypnotherapy training in Issaquah, Washington. With trained helpers supporting us, we added wood to the booming fire that we'd eventually be invited to walk across in our bare feet. After sunset, when the fire became hot coals, our teachers asked us to be fully grounded in our bodies. We were instructed to determine if it was safe to walk across the fire. The lesson wasn't about walking on fire. The experience was about trusting our inner knowing. I remember going deep inside myself, pulling my arms in close, breathing, and scanning my body from head to toe. My body, via intuitive heart intelligence, gave me a clear yes, and I walked purposefully and carefully across the hot coals. We were later given a baggy filled with ashes from our fire. The walkers and the watchers each received sacred cinders, along with a written message that read: I Trust My Inner Knowing.

Research has shown that the heart sends powerful signals to the brain and the rest of the body. These heart signals help us to self-regulate our emotions and nervous systems. I was regulating my nervous system when I went "deep inside myself, pulling my arms in close, breathing, and scanning my body from head to toe." I recognized and honored my heart's signal that it was safe to walk across the fire, so I did something I never thought I could do. Core heart feelings generate heart signals that align our minds and emotions, giving more intuitive clarity (my clear yes) and more strength and energy to achieve our goals.

My recovery is about discerning what information, program, product, doctor, food is right for me. I fully trust my inner knowing. This heart wisdom is a resource on my journey. As you read the rest of my story and about the other birth issues below,[11,12] I invite you to discern. This is an opportunity to strengthen your relationship with your inner knowing.

Note: The charts on the following pages combine information taught during my hypnotherapy and breathwork training. The words "never," and "always," occasionally appear in the relationship and individual issues columns. This does not mean that the challenges *always/never* occur. For example, "never feels love for him/herself" is an absolute that doesn't allow for a continuum, context, or for healing.

"You're not a victim for sharing your story. You are a survivor setting the world on fire with your truth. And you never know who needs your light, your warmth and raging courage."

\- Alex Elle

BIRTHS/ EXPERIENCES IN UTERO	RELATIONSHIP ISSUES	INDIVIDUAL ISSUES	BELIEFS
Twins	Come here-go away, space invaders, who was born first, codependency, separation, when one twin dies in utero or birth	Who am I?	
Caesarean	Expects to be rescued, takes the easy way out, difficulty overcoming obstacles, boundary invaders, strongly reacts to boundary violations, may resent authority figures, no follow through	Often cut on themselves May do self-mutilation such as body rings, tattoos, drug usage	I can't do it myself, I'm doing it wrong, I am damned if I do and damned if I don't
Anesthetic birth	Codependency—feels powerless, expects emotional abandon-ment, difficulty bonding	Addictions: usage of pot, cocaine, heroin, caffeine, disassociation, often goes numb	I'm always in a fog, I fade in and out, I feel dead, I feel ungrounded, disconnected, smothered, I feel spacey, I feel cold (emotionally)
Forceps	Authority rebellion, often feels violated	Headaches, lack of personal power	Men/women hurt me, I can't do it by myself
Pitocin		Feel overwhelmed, powerless	
Stuck in birth canal	Fear of intimacy, often feels suffo-cated	May have breathing difficulties: bronchitis, asthma, emphysema, pneumonia, often smokes	

BIRTHS/ EXPERIENCES IN UTERO	RELATIONSHIP ISSUES	INDIVIDUAL ISSUES	BELIEFS
Breech	Rescues others, the victim triangle, feels responsible for others' pain, puts others' pain first, ignores own needs altogether, takes on guilt for other people's pain, extreme people-pleaser (adaptive)	Conflicted about moving forward or making changes, spends a lot of unnecessary energy struggling	I am always doing things wrong, I don't know which way to go, I am always doing things backward
Abortion considered, abortion survivor	Fear of abandonment, codependency, extreme people-pleaser, fear of commitment	Death urge, suicide thoughts/ attempts, never good enough, feels impotent, anxiety disorder; terror of annihilation, pervasive shame, "to be or not to be" existential angst, life is always a double bind, shame an existential issue	Life is scary; someone is trying to kill me, life hurts, I don't want to live
Familial/ cultural desire for other sex (gender prejudice)	Fear of abandonment, Never accepts love	Always feels inadequate, extreme people-pleaser, sexual identity confusion, transvestite, gender confusion, anxiety disorder, terror of annihilation, pervasive shame	I am a disappoint-ment, I am confused (one parent wanted a boy, the other a girl), I should be a boy/girl(decision made by child about their sexuality), I am the wrong one, I'll never make others happy
Test tube babies		Who am I?	
Induced births			I can't get started, I can't get what I want

BIRTHS/ EXPERIENCES IN UTERO	RELATIONSHIP ISSUES	INDIVIDUAL ISSUES	BELIEFS

PARENTAL FEARS

Not enough money for the child		Child grows up with great financial anxiety, never succeeding financially, feels the need to justify existence	
Something is wrong with the baby		Generalized anxiety disorder	
Mother will die from childbirth		Overpowering fears of death, abandonment, annihilation, Mother may hold onto child to prevent birth, suffocation issues, always holding back, afraid to move forward	Held back births, I can't get what I want when I want it, others are holding me back, I must leave to prevent others from holding me back
Any fears of parents		May become anxiety/panic disorder	
Drug Usage _alcohol, tobacco, pot, cocaine, caffeine, heroin, crack, etc._		A drug-dependent child, mood swings, may look bi-polar	

FAMILIAL CONDITIONS AT TIME OF BIRTH

Unwelcome child _not wanted, a disappointment_	May recreate rejection, highly adaptive (the adaptive smile)		

BIRTHS/ EXPERIENCES IN UTERO	RELATIONSHIP ISSUES	INDIVIDUAL ISSUES	BELIEFS

FAMILIAL CONDITIONS AT TIME OF BIRTH

BIRTHS/ EXPERIENCES IN UTERO	RELATIONSHIP ISSUES	INDIVIDUAL ISSUES	BELIEFS
Given up for adoption	Abandonment anxiety, sells their soul for love, rebellious to authority, fear of commitment	Death urge, depression, shame, highly adaptive, difficulty bonding	
The replace-ment child *Mother may have lost hus-band, parent, another child, sibling*	Never feels love for him/ her self, highly competitive, highly adaptive (the adaptive smile), love feels suf-focating, always trying to be someone else, jealousy, envy, difficulty bonding	Overwhelming lack of self-esteem, constant feeling of inadequacy, lifelong grief, unexplained depression, identity disorder—never has own identity	
Unwanted, unplanned "illegitimate" births			I am not wanted, I don't deserve to be here/be alive, no one wants me
"Spousified" child	Rescues and caretakes others, may have sexual/emotional loyalty to parent which prevents commitment to life partner, tied to mother's apron strings, codependent	Doesn't know how to play, overly responsible, feels highly inadequate, intense sense of pressure	
Post-partum separation			They don't want me, I must have done something wrong, I can't get what I want, I must be worthless, my needs will never be met

REFLECTIONS

I've shared that my heroine's journey includes discernment about the impact of traumatic events surrounding birth on my beliefs and both individual and relationship issues. As I began to reflect, I saw a pattern emerging in that first set of beliefs recorded during my hypnotherapy session.

Thoughts that I was betrayed and abandoned, it was my fault, my twin died of starvation, I'm not safe, and even I ate my vanishing twin show a pattern of all-or-nothing thinking. That thinking runs through the faulty beliefs that I took on before I was born. I saw things in extremes. I'm either good or bad. It's either my fault or it isn't. I know in my head that all-or-nothing thinking has long been associated with disordered eating.

Black-and-white thinking is also known as dichotomous thinking. It's a cognitive distortion where individuals see things in extremes with no middle ground. Author Julia Zakrzewski, explains that this type of thinking can play a significant role in the development and mainte-nance of disordered eating behaviors.[13] She describes the impact of dichotomous thinking on behavior.[14]

All-or-Nothing Attitudes: Individuals with disordered eating might see their eating habits as either completely good or bad. I fall into this trap. If I feel like I've blown it—a meal, a diet, missing a day of exercise—I often feel like I've completely failed. This feeling can trigger binging food, TV, shopping—you name it.

Body Image Distortion: Individuals with body image distortion may view their bodies in extreme terms, seeing themselves as either perfect or disgusting. This can lead to unhealthy behaviors aimed at achieving an unrealistic body image. I avoid mirrors and having my picture taken. The critic in my head uses words like disgusting and repulsive. These feelings are so painful that they can trigger binging.

Control Issues: Black-and-white thinking can contribute to a need for control. Strict dietary rules and rigid exercise routines can provide a false sense of control. They also set individuals up for feelings of failure and guilt when they inevitably deviate from these rules. I always perceived myself as easygoing, a go-with-the-flow, low-maintenance, easy-to-live-and-work-with person. I was surprised at one point when a friend said I was wound tight! I can see how using control was an attempt to feel safe. Feelings of guilt and failure are too much to handle. These feelings have triggered binge behavior.

Emotional Responses: This type of thinking can lead to intense emotional responses and impulsive behaviors. For instance, a small deviation from a diet plan might trigger a binge-eating episode, followed by feelings of shame and guilt, perpetuating a cycle of extremes. Awareness is the first step in breaking the cycle.

I believe that as I increase my nuanced or dialectical thinking, I'll experience a more balanced and realistic understanding of the world. Developing this habit of thought will foster open-mindedness and adaptability.

I am now able to acknowledge that my perinatal experience was a traumatic event, that some basic needs were not met, and that I was often in a state of shock. It makes sense that trauma happened *inside* me because of what happened to me. I occasionally experience disconnection from my emotions, difficulty staying in the present moment, and negative views of myself and others.

This realization is not a judgment about my parents, caregivers in the hospital, or the medical system. In the coming years, I expect we'll better understand the needs of mothers and babies and design policies and practices that support their feelings of safety and connection from the start.

It's important to acknowledge that even though I have a birth narrative, I am not my birth story!

NOTES

1. Brent Babcock. *My Twin Vanished: Did Yours? The Vanishing Twin Crisis.* (London: Tate Publishing & Enterprises, LLC, 2009).
2. Cleveland Clinic. "Vanishing Twin Syndrome." 2022. https://my.clevelandclinic.org/.
3. Brook. *Birth's Hidden Legacy.* 41.
4. American Psychiatric Association. *Diagnostic and Statistical Manual of Mental Disorders.* (Washington, DC: American Psychiatric Association, 1994).
5. Brook. *Birth's Hidden Legacy.* 41.
6. B. Van der Kolk. *The Body Keeps the Score: Brain, Mind, and Body in the Healing of Trauma.* (New York: Viking Press, 2014).
7. Carol A. Lampman. *Integration Concepts, Level One Professional Training Manual.* https://www.integrationconcepts.net/.
8. Lampman. *Integration Concepts, Level One Professional Training Manual.*
9. The Wellness Institute. *Birth Issues: Hypnotherapy Training Manual.* (2010) https://www.wellness-institute.org/
10. Brook. *Birth's Hidden Legacy.* 41.

11. Lampman. *Integration Concepts, Level One Professional Training Manual.*

12. Julia Zakrzewski. "Understanding and Breaking the Binge Restrict Cycle." (2023) https://www.usenourish.com/blog/binge-restrict-cycle.

13. Zakrzewski. "Understanding and Breaking the Binge Restrict Cycle."

14. Zakrzewski. "Understanding and Breaking the Binge Restrict Cycle."

CHAPTER 4
A PICTURE'S WORTH A THOUSAND WORDS

A friend noticed that I look incredibly sad in many pictures from my childhood. I hadn't noticed that before. My story has always been that my childhood was ideal, and the world was awesome. I'm proud to be an optimist. I see the world through rose-colored glasses and find the good in every situation. And this is an illusion, a reality I've created to avoid experiencing the sad, the uncomfortable, the scary, the unspeakable.

Here are some of the hurts I've stuffed inside and now have presented themselves for healing.

I was the little girl in the picture above when mom said, "If you keep eating like that you'll be as big as a barn." I was this little girl when the neighbor said, "You're too fat to play in our tree house." I was this little girl when the ballet teacher said, "You're too fat to be a ballerina." I was this little girl when another neighbor called me a red-faced mop top. I was this little girl and didn't know that I was exactly right. I was this little girl who took spare change from the junk drawer to buy Pine Brothers™ chewy cough drops, which I ate like candy. I was this young girl when I was demoted to the lowest reading group. I was this little girl who was embarrassed by the stylish clothes my mom wore and hated the hats she made me wear. I was a young pre-teen when a friend of the family sexually molested me.

I am this young girl. I was happy, adventurous, grateful, worried, anxious, angry, resentful, ashamed, excited, motivated, rageful, disappointed, embarrassed, curious, and grief-stricken. I buried the negative feelings and became a people-pleasing Pollyanna who spent a lot of energy not rocking the boat. I took on the persona of a clown, using humor to lighten things up. I made efforts to control our family dynamics by being good and maintaining peace.

Dr. Anita Johnston's best-selling book, *Eating in the Light of the Moon*, has been incredibly helpful in my quest to understand and heal the mysterious obsession I experience with food, eating, hunger, and body image. She writes:

"I learned that as very young girls, these women were bright and gifted and had an exceptional ability to perceive subtle realities. More often than not, a woman who struggled with disordered eating was once a girl who saw the invisible, who read between the lines, who sensed when things were not right. She noticed when people said one thing but did another. She could discern certain patterns of behavior and anticipate what was going to come next... she received a very clear message (often nonverbal) that (this) outspoken and questioning behavior was not okay and even dangerous to the stability of the family."[1]

I am this little girl who wanted to stomp her feet, scream, punch someone, throw something, and run away. I couldn't rock the boat, so all the energy that didn't come out stayed stuck in my body until I was ready to heal. And boy, did I kick, scream, and rage!

REFLECTIONS

My heroine's journey includes getting to know my younger self, the sad little girl in the pictures. Tracie Pedersen and Jamie Smith describe this therapy as inner child work.[2] Inner child work is a powerful therapeutic practice that helps you connect with and heal the wounded parts of your younger self. It involves acknowledging and addressing past experiences and emotions that might be affecting your present life. The "inner child" refers to the part of your psyche that retains the feelings, memories, and experiences of your childhood.

Over time, I've developed a loving relationship with Little Laura. Not everyone can relate to inner child work. I get it. The important concept is that we all have wounds from childhood that influence our beliefs, relationships, and self-concept. Working with your inner child can help you understand and heal from past traumas, unmet needs, and emotional pain.

A beloved core energetics[3] practitioner once asked me who would make the first move when I started dating again. I looked puzzled. He replied, "Little Laura, she'll be saying, see me, see me, hug me, hug me, love me, love me, and she'll run up to your date and throw her arms around him." I recognized that pattern of behavior in my adult life! I acknowledge that Little Laura needs to feel safe and connected. It's my job as an adult to reassure younger, wounded parts of me that I am safe and I am loved. My wise, adult self is now front and center, making healthy decisions on my behalf.

Along my journey, I've come to understand that we are energy and that managing our energy is critical to our wellbeing. The little girl in the picture didn't understand that emotions are energy in motion inside her body. She wasn't aware of the connection between physical and emotional health and the importance of feeling her uncomfortable feelings. Like many people, I believe that emotional trauma (like sexual abuse) causes tension and stuck energy in the body.

Our survival instincts kick in when we feel threatened. Olivia Guy Evans, MSc, helps us understand how our autonomic nervous system activates the fight, flight, freeze, or fawn response.[4]

Fight: Preparing to confront the threat directly. This involves increased adrenaline, muscle tension, and heightened awareness. Little Laura (and adult Laura as well) didn't kick, punch, stomp her feet, or fight back with words when she was hurt. Some of the pent-up energy remains stuck inside of me. Much of the stuck energy has been slowly released through hypnotherapy, breathwork, trauma release exercises, and movement. I have a damn it doll, a stress-relief tool designed to help vent frustrations. The idea is to whack the doll against a surface when feeling stressed or angry instead of taking it out on yourself or others. I collaborated with a team that bought dolls that were used in this way to release pent-up energy at work. An inexpensive and straightforward way to release anger, frustration, and stress is to scream in the car or somewhere out in nature. The point is to get the extra energy out of your body to regulate your nervous system.

Flight: The instinct to run away from the threat. This response can make your heart race, breathing quicken, and energy surge, all to help you escape danger. The wounded child and adult parts of me found ways to take flight. As a child, I'd hide in my room. As an adult, I'd get far away from the emotionally threatening boyfriend, spouse, boss, or colleague. When I experienced sexual abuse, I didn't take flight or fight back. As a young person, I didn't have the resources to act. I've worked with a counselor who uses body movement to help sexually abused clients like me release stored trauma.

Freeze: Sometimes, the body might freeze when it perceives a threat. This can be a way of becoming less noticeable or preparing to decide the next best action. On my journey, I've learned that dissociation has been one of my freeze responses as a child and as an adult. I have creative ways to disconnect from painful thoughts, feelings, or sense of identity. There is a connection between addiction and the freeze response to threat. When people experience chronic stress or trauma, their nervous system can become dysregulated, leading to a state of hypoarousal or freeze.

Fawn: Gina Ryder explains, "This is a trauma response where an individual tries to appease or please others to avoid conflict and maintain a sense of safety. This behavior often stems from childhood trauma, where pleasing an abusive or neglectful parent or authority figure was a survival strategy." [5]

My journey has helped me see more clearly how much time and energy I've expended trying to please others and to avoid conflict. I hid or split off from the authentic parts of myself that know how to speak the truth, feel empowered, manage conflict, and set boundaries. Fawning may well be my most automatic trauma response. I am feeling compassion for the part of me that has turned to addictive behaviors to cope with emotional turmoil.

I'm finding that understanding these responses has been incredibly empowering. I'm finding ways to manage stress and anxiety more effectively.

NOTES

1. Anita Johnston, Anita. *Eating in the Light of the Moon: How Women Can Transform Their Relationships with Food Through Myths, Metaphors and Storytelling.* (Carlsbad, CA: Gurza Books, 1996) xiv.

2. Tracie Pederson and Jamie Smith. "10 Exercises to Heal Your Inner Child." 2022. https://psychcentral.com/health/how-to-heal-your-inner-child.

3. The Institute of Core Energetics. https://www.coreenergetics.org/.

4. Olivia Guy Evans. "Fight, Flight, Freeze, or Fawn: How We Respond to Threats." 2023. https://www.simplypsychology.org/fight-flight-freeze-fawn.html.

5. Gina Ryder. "The Fawn Response: How Trauma Can Lead to People-Pleasing." 2022. https://psychcentral.com/health/fawn-response.

CHAPTER 5
MY NERVOUS SYSTEM BREAKDOWN

My first panic attack happened early one morning in front of a group of nuns and other students earning their school principal certification. I was a guest presenter invited to talk about engaging parents in meaningful ways with the school community. Several minutes into the talk, my face went numb, and I found myself unable to speak. I excused myself and hurried out of the room. The instructor followed me to the drinking fountain and asked if I was okay. "Sure," I said, "I'm just lightheaded." I took a deep breath, numbed my anxiety, ignored the signals my body was sending me, pulled myself together, and headed back into the room, poised as the expert. I told the group that I hadn't eaten breakfast and I was fine.

I was grateful that the first group to witness my vulnerability happened to be a group of nuns who held out their hands as if to catch me should I begin to pass out. This was the beginning of my deep dive into depression and anxiety. It was humbling to experience my body doing things that were out of my control: hands and legs shaking, palsy-like freezing in my face, lips going numb, and the inability to calm my breath. I began to fear what I loved most, teaching and leading groups. What if I panicked again?

Within a few days, I panicked while driving my daughters and two friends to the movies. I knew that something terrible was going to happen. I took the kids home and drove myself to urgent care. This is common for those who experience panic attacks; they seem to come out of nowhere. People often feel that they are about to have a heart attack. The doctor prescribed Xanax and suggested that I see a therapist.

As a researcher, I realize that context matters. All the things that happen around us, our environment, our responses, and reactions to people, places, and situations influence our mental, physical, emotional, and spiritual wellbeing. I was forty years old, raising two teenage daughters as a single parent, waiting for the results of a funky pap smear, in a relationship with a man on the verge of breaking up with me, and halfway through a doctoral program in urban education. I quit my job and became a teaching assistant, in hopes of finishing my dissertation quickly. I planned to become a university professor and to send both girls to college for free.

My boyfriend and I talked about selling everything and opening a bed and breakfast at the foot of the mountains in a neighboring state. We'd be married. He'd run the horse farm on the property. The kids would love this life. We'd continue to ride snowmobiles, hike in the woods, ride the motorcycle, and meet people from all over the world. I'd finish my dissertation in this peaceful place, surrounded by a national forest.

My body gave me clues for several months that something was not right. I continued to have panic attacks, experienced depression and anxiety, felt numbness in my face and tingling in my arms, and I kept my man-friend. I now understand that my heart and my brain were not aligned. What I was thinking (*How exciting! We'll get married and run a B & B!*) and what I was feeling (*I know in my heart that this is not a healthy relationship*) were not congruent.

Here's the kicker. I'm afraid of horses, there were no urban schools nearby, and my daughters would spend their teenage years away from family, friends, and schools they loved. More importantly, deep in my heart, beneath the armor and buried under layer upon layer of fear, shame, anger, rage, jealousy, sadness, and grief—feelings that had been pushed down over the years—was a knowing. This was not a healthy relationship; my needs weren't being met, and neither were his. I was not living my truth. I could not and should not will this relationship to work.

Running out on a group of nuns on a sunny morning, the sense that something terrible would happen had I kept driving to the movie theatre, waking up to the reality that my heart and mind were out of alignment, leaving me in an incoherent state, and my entire BE-ing experiencing a nervous breakdown, stopped me in my tracks.

I did not plan to have a nervous system breakdown. It was my body's signal to pay attention. My sympathetic and parasympathetic nervous systems were out of whack. It was also my first lesson (a recurring one, I might add) in surrender and the act of letting go. My need to just breathe for a while and get it together before getting out of bed each morning was my version of hitting rock bottom.

REFLECTIONS

I've studied in a sacred mystery school for more than a decade. One of the concepts introduced early on is known as maya. Maya is often translated as "illusion" or "magic" and refers to the belief that the world we perceive with our senses is an illusion, obscuring the true nature of reality. My nervous system breakdown is my way of sharing how I came to better understand maya and illusion. I created a story (illusion) that things were great. My nervous system breakdown enabled me to slow down and to see the reality of my situation.

Learning to recognize and treat shock and trauma was part of my hypnotherapy and breathwork training. Gaining a deeper under-standing of these concepts has helped me make connections between my challenges with food and hunger and the work of my autonomic nervous system. I hope this will assist you on your journey as well.

Shock: Shock is trauma entrenched in the nervous system. It's a natural reaction to an overwhelming and distressing experience. It's your body's way of protecting you from the full emotional impact of the traumatic event right away. My hypnotherapy teachers taught me how to recognize shock. "We can see shock in the eyes of those who stare blankly, who talk incessantly, and who go through life not present in their bodies. People in parasympathetic (paralyzed) shock usually seek out stimulants such as excessive caffeine drinks and drugs such as cocaine or stimulants such as methamphetamines. People in sympathetic (frantic behavior) shock usually seek out more calming drugs such as alcohol, pot, antidepressants, or sugar." [1]

My body went into a state of shock in front of the nuns as I was teaching. I wasn't fully aware of the trauma. I was not in a healthy relationship. It wouldn't make sense to move my daughters away from their school and friends. I was worried about my finances. I was having a delayed reaction. My mind might have initially shielded me from the emotional pain, but my body still reacted with symptoms of shock.

Trauma: According to Rachel Lewis-Marlow of the Embodied Recovery Institute, "Embodied recovery is a trauma-informed approach to treating eating disorders that emphasizes the connection between eating, attachment, and trauma. It utilizes a somatic-based method to help individuals regulate emotions and connect with others, fostering a supportive environment for recovery. This approach is grounded in the latest research in traumatology and inter-personal neurobiology, aiming to address the physiological and rela-tional aspects of eating disorders."[2]

Paula Scatoloni, helps us see the connection between eating, attach-ment, and trauma. "Individuals struggling to express fight energy manifest it through purging, chewing, and spitting, anger turned on the body, and self-harm behaviors."[3] My fight response was activated as I was aggressively trying to solve a problem. I was making efforts to repair what clearly wasn't working (suggesting counseling, trying to change my behavior) in an attempt to salvage the relationship with my boyfriend.

My personal and professional experiences have shown me that indi-viduals who experience stuck flight energy will present with anxiety, panic, obsessive thoughts, food rituals, binge eating, or excessive exer-cise. [4] My flight response centered on avoidance and withdrawal. I ignored the issues, avoided discussions, and distanced myself physi-cally. After several months of panic attacks, depression, and anxiety, I finally withdrew completely from the relationship.

The freeze response involves a sense of disembodiment (dissociation, numbing), inability to track fullness or hunger, inability to engage in relationships, and depressed mood.[5] I was forty years old when I experienced my nervous system breakdown. My journey with depression had begun.

I've learned that turning to food for comfort during times of stress or shock is quite common. Often, individuals who struggle with disordered eating manifest all the above, shifting from one nervous system state to another on any given day.

Having a nervous system breakdown has helped me to recognize and address illusion, shock, and trauma. This experience also taught me about **coherence**,[6] the alignment of the heart, brain, hormones, and nervous system. I witnessed firsthand the physical, emotional, mental, and spiritual impact of being out of coherence or in an incoherent state." It's our heart coherence that makes it easier to sustain emotional commitment, reduce stress, and create healthier eating habits."[7]

When what we think (mind) and how we truly feel (heart) are aligned, we are in a state of balance, and our physical, mental, emotional, and spiritual systems are good to go. When our thoughts and feelings are out of alignment, our bodies do everything possible to get our attention!

I've been teaching and practicing HeartMath™ techniques for a long time. I'm so inspired by their work to "help people connect with the guidance of their own hearts to improve emotional wellbeing, reduce stress, and enhance overall health,"[8] that I became a certified Resilience Advantage Trainer®.[9]

"Resilience is the capacity to prepare for, recover from and adapt in the face of stress, challenge or adversity."
-Institute of HeartMath™

NOTES

1. Zimberoff and Hartman. *Overcoming Shock: Healing the Traumatized Mind and Heart.*

2. Rachel Lewis-Marlow. Episode 20 Embodied Approach to Eating Disorders. 2022. https://embodiedrecovery.org/.

3. Paula Scatoloni. "Understanding the Connection Between Eating, Attachment, and Trauma." 2021. https://embodiedrecovery.org/.

4. Institute of HeartMath™. *Resilience Advantage™ Guidebook.* 2014. https://www.heartmath.org/.

5. Childre and Rozman. *Stopping Emotional Eating.* 27-53.

6. Institute of HeartMath™. *Resilience Advantage™ Guidebook.*

7. Institute of HeartMath™. *Resilience Advantage™ Guidebook.*

8. Institute of HeartMath™. *Resilience Advantage™ Guidebook.*

9. Institute of HeartMath™. *Resilience Advantage™ Guidebook.*

CHAPTER 6

HANNA, MY DELTA GAMMA

Hanna, My Delta Gamma

"Hanna, my Delta Gamma,
She's got a figure like a baby grand piana
She's not so nifty, she weighs two fifty,

But fat girls now and then are relished by the best of men.
Oh Hanna, my Delta Gamma,
I put my arms around as far as they will go, go, go,
Oh, I don't care for pretty faces,
All I want is Hanna's graces,
Hanna my Delta Gamma!"[1]

Pledging Delta Gamma (DG) was one of the highlights of my undergraduate experience at Wittenberg University. I came across this picture circa 1977 or 1978 during an alumni homecoming weekend several years ago. I was immediately struck by what I now recognize as a face and body in a trance or a dissociative state. I was serving myself food with my hands and I was not at all present with my surroundings. I have a far-away look in my eyes. Wearing a hoodie at the dinner table is not something I ever remember doing. This picture is worth a thousand words in my quest to understand my binge-eating behavior.

The story of my vanishing twin brought to light many possibilities about my quest for peace around food and hunger based on information held in my unconscious or subconscious mind. My experiences and beliefs were *internal* in nature. The song "Hanna, My Delta Gamma" is external, and a fitting example, among millions, of the ways a toxic culture impacts distorted eating and body image. For years, I participated in singing a song that "othered," judged, and shamed an imaginary girl because of her body size. I laughed and danced with others in circles and pretended that I/we loved her anyway.

I started smoking in college. Cigarette smoking took the place of snacking and gave my mouth something to do. I smoked on the way to the pool to swim laps. Exercising, smoking, restricting, and binging became strategies for not becoming a fat girl. I wanted to be relished by the best of men looking lean and sexy.

A few years ago, I sang this song publicly while assisting a hypnotherapy cohort in training. This helped me release the deep shame that I had been holding on to. Shame is a dense, low vibration emotion. As mentioned before, emotions are energy in motion. Emotions aren't good or bad. I've learned that we want to recognize and feel our emotions and find ways to let these energies in motion flow through and out of our bodies. Staying stuck in low vibrational emotions like shame, guilt, grief, and anger can result in sickness and feelings of powerlessness. As humans, we feel (feelings) a wide range of energies (emotions) in our bodies. These are cues about our sense of balance and wellbeing. Many of us have been conditioned by our families of origin, churches, and culture to carry shame. We feel guilty when we believe that we've done something wrong. We feel shame when we believe that there is something wrong with us.

When we believe at our core, in the internal, invisible landscape of BE-ing, that something is wrong with us, we accept craziness, drama, and chaos into our lives. We are innately wired for safety and connection. Shame does not feel safe and impacts our ability to connect with others in healthy ways.

The *Barbie* movie was released in 2023. The film follows Barbie and Ken as they embark on a journey of self-discovery, traveling from the perfect world of Barbieland to the real world.[2] Many moviegoers dressed in pink and wore *Barbie* accessories. Following the release of the movie, I read about controversies that surround *Barbie* and how several women have stepped up to challenge the toxic, body-shaming, diet-focused, unrealistic standards of beauty that women and girls (I should include men and boys here as well) are bombarded with daily.

"Girls see female body images everywhere today and it's critical that parents and caregivers provide perspective on what they are seeing," a Mattel spokesperson said in an email to Today.com. "It's important to remember that Barbie is a doll who stands 11.5 inches tall and weighs 7.25 ounces — she was never modeled on the proportions of a real person." [3]

Nickolay Lamm, an artist, recently changed Barbie's proportions, creating a 3-D image of a new Barbie prototype that would more accurately depict a nineteen-year-old's body. "Lamm created the image using Photoshop and the Centers for Disease Control's measurements of an average nineteen-year-old woman. The new and improved Barbie appears shorter and wider than the previous version, has bigger feet, and has even come down off her tippy toes to stand more comfortably flat-footed." Lamm writes, "I created normal Barbie because I wanted to show that average is beautiful."[4]

Another artist, Galia Slaven, recovering from anorexia, created a life-sized Barbie that made her debut several years ago at Hamilton College. The college was the first to introduce Eating Disorder Awareness Week on campus. The life-sized creation was meant to symbolize Slaven's own recovery and bring awareness to the disease. "My Barbie's role is simple," Slayen said. "She grabs the attention of apathetic onlookers and makes them think and talk about an issue that thrives in silence." [5]

I hope Mattel and others will be motivated to create realistic dolls that reflect diversity in size, race and ethnicity, hobbies, career aspirations, cultural accessories, and artifacts.

Our needs for safety and connection are so powerful that many of us are willing to sacrifice our authenticity to fit in. I acknowledge that I've been swept up in and have contributed to the toxic beauty culture. My story is like *The Ugly Duckling*. In middle school, a boy in history class turned around and told me that I was the ugliest girl he'd ever seen. I was teased for being five feet, eight inches tall. Boys made fun of my large, swollen lips. The swan in me (according to cultural beauty standards) began to emerge in high school. I sat alongside the homecoming queen as her junior-year attendant. Weeks before the start of my first year in college, I was voted "one of the sexiest butts" at water safety instructor camp. I had a brief modeling career in the summer when I was laid off as an elementary school teacher. The full-page spread in the newspaper was titled "Sultry and Sexy." For a long time, much of my identity was centered on my looks.

Tracking down the author and timeline of *Hanna, My Delta Gamma*, has been interesting. I've learned that she may not have been created by the sorority. I recently had a great talk with the Delta Gamma archivist at the Executive Office. She let me know that many sorority records, including the song handbooks, have been shipped out of state to be digitalized. For the time being, I don't know if, when, or why the song may have been discontinued. I'm inspired to explore the impact of the song on generations of young women over the last 70 years. The archivist was supportive of this project and encouraged me to reach out to the publisher of our DG magazine and share my story.

"Trying to escape media influences in today's culture is as feasible as trying to protect ourselves from air pollution by not breathing."
-Brené Brown

REFLECTIONS

During my hypnotherapy training, I was introduced to a new concept that has helped me understand how what happened to me is held as trauma inside of me. If "Hanna My Delta Gamma" was a real live woman, not a character, this idea would resonate with her as well. Let me introduce you to a concept called **Need-Shock, Need-Shame.**

Have you ever seen kittens spooning in a basket? Maybe you've experienced the awesomeness of spooning with a beloved other. All mammals are biologically wired to need safety and connection. We wouldn't spoon or face away from someone unless we felt safe with them, unless we knew they had our back. Without having to think about it, our bodies are constantly scanning our internal and external environments for safety and connection. As infants, we cry when we need something or someone. When our needs aren't met, we begin to lose trust in the people and world around us. We lose our sense of safety and connection and find a variety of ways to soothe ourselves. Loving our blanket, sucking a thumb, and rocking are learned behaviors that help us regulate in healthy ways. When babies lose trust in their caregivers and develop fears about expressing their needs, they learn to regulate in unhealthy ways, they stop expressing or "having needs," and they learn to shut down.

This really happened! During a hypnotherapy-psychodrama session, I age-regressed to the incubator. The facilitator therapist, along with other client helpers, often uses props and your exact language (a linguistic bridge) during a psychodrama. To recreate the sounds, lighting, and machines associated with an incubator, the team placed a small fan near my mat on the floor. I immediately bonded with the fan by moving closer to it and staying there throughout the session. It is possible that in the absence of my mother, I sought comfort in the machines, sounds, and sensations that surrounded me.

Adults have needs as well. Triggering people or events activates our immediate shock response via the parasympathetic or sympathetic nervous system. When the immediate shock response becomes unbearable, we attempt to use compensating addictive behaviors or substances. When we attempt abstinence from the compensating addiction, we experience shame (I am bad), which triggers the immediate shock response again. It's easy to see how need-shock and need-shame contribute to the binge and restrict cycle that so many of us experience when we diet.

The autonomic nervous system (ANS) is the part of your nervous system that works automatically (without conscious effort) to regulate vital functions like heart rate, digestion, respiratory rate, and more. It has two main parts: The sympathetic nervous system activates the fight or flight response to prepare your body for action during stress. The parasympathetic nervous system controls the rest and digest functions to bring your body back to a calm state.

These systems work together to keep your body in balance, adjusting as needed to internal and external conditions.

When we feel bored, numb, exhausted, discouraged, or depressed for example, we may experience *parasympathetic shock*. Our breathing cycles per minute decrease, our parasympathetic shock increases, and our coherence decreases as we move from boredom to depression. I've been taught that "when in parasympathetic shock, we self-medicate by activating the sympathetic nervous system. Compensating addictions or patterns of behavior include shopping, coffee, sex, binging and uppers." [6]

When we feel restlessness, drama, ADHD, anxiety, or panic, for example, we may experience *sympathetic shock*. Our breathing cycles per minute increase, our sympathetic shock increases, and our coherence decreases as we move from restlessness to panic. When in sympathetic shock, we self-medicate by activating the parasympathetic nervous system. Compensating addictions or patterns of behavior include food, alcohol, sleep, sex, technology, and down-ers." [7]

Need-Shock, Need-Shame Cycle and Disordered Eating

Restriction leads to feelings of deprivation, hunger, loneliness, and emptiness. To cope or escape the pain of unmet needs, the individual turns to the familiar habit of binging, and the cycle begins again.

As humans, we become creative when our needs for safety and connection are not met. Most often, we aren't even conscious of the unmet need. We engage in unwanted behaviors (smoking, gambling, overeating) to survive. On some level, I believe that my connection to Hanna and the certainty that her story is my story and that it must be told, springs from my inner knowing that it's time to rediscover the feminine. There's more for me to explore here!

"Women who struggle with disordered eating, more often than not have an overly dominant masculine aspect that continually attempts to control the inner feminine. Their masculine side is unrelentingly critical, even hostile, toward their feminine side." [7]
-Anita Johnston

Personal Soul Collage Card: The Struggle

Postscript

Spring 2025

Context matters. Historical timeframes, geographical locations, social and cultural norms, gender, socioeconomic status, etc., each influence our stories. I've recently learned that "Hanna My Delta Gamma" (sister does not use an h at the end of her name in this song) is not a Delta Gamma song at all! It was created by a man (or men) in a male fraternity sometime between 1930-1950. Delta Gamma Fraternity (the women's organization's legal name) began copyrighting songs in 1888! One of their traditional songs, "Well, Well, Well, Hannah," lyrics by Barbara Laederach, is sung to the same tune as "Hanna My Delta Gamma." The lyrics, however, carry quite different messages. The sociocultural differences between the women's version and the men's creation/interpretation are worth adding this postscript to my story. This is verse one of "Well, Well, Well, Hannah" found in a Delta Gamma Songbook.

Well, well, well Hannah, My Delta Gamma,

She's playing real hot tunes around her old her piana,

She's really nifty,

She plays so swiftly,

That now a days it's hard to keep the men away from her.

Well , well, well, Hannah, my Delta Gamma,

Oh, how I long to tell her that I love her so, so, so!

I don't go for other's faces,

I just go for Hannah's graces,

Hannah, my Delta Gamma.

The following comments about the men's version, "Hanna My Delta Gamma," part of a thread found on the Mudcat Café Music Foundation website (https://mudcat.org/), give us some insight into perceptions about beauty in a particular culture over time. At this time, it seemed okay to objectify a woman based on her weight. Songs were viewed as a way to tease. Perhaps if it's silly, it won't hurt so much or sound as mean, and we see that women (and I'm one of them) participated in what we now call body shaming or fat shaming.

"The idea of Hannah first surfaced in an old vaudeville hit, 'Hannah from Indiana' by P.H., Wilson, (who would later become a DG Dad). The familiar Delta Gamma song, 'Hanna' has been sung since the 1930s."

"I heard this at the University of Idaho about 1948. But they sang 'stylish stout' instead of 'fat.'"

"The second verse of the song: 'Well look at Hanna, She's got a man-a, She's loosing weight all around her fann-a, She's getting nifty, She's lost one-fifty, And now it's hard to keep the boys away from my Hannah, my Delta Gamma, Oh how I long to tell her that I love her so, so, so, so, I don't care for pretty faces, I just long for Hannah's graces, Hanna! My Delta Gamma!' My father used to sing it to me when I was a little girl. His lyrics were slightly different. His version had 'fat girls are prized by the best of men' for example, but it's definitely the same song, and I used to sing it to my kids as I put them to bed. Dad would have learned it at University of Kansas in the 1940s."[8]

You can probably tell that I have empathy for Hanna and have a great deal of compassion for myself for body shaming that I took on from the culture, from others and mostly from my inner critic. I'm interested in hearing stories from women and men who may have taken on shame that Hanna likely would have carried for being overweight, and from those who may better understand the impact of these words knowing more about the increasing numbers of people who struggle with disordered eating.

Eating disorders affect both women and men, though the prevalence is higher among women. Approximately 8.6% of women and 4.07% of men experience an eating disorder at some point in their lives.[9]

NOTES

1. John Frushour and Deborrah Schefferli. "Hanna, My Delta Gamma." 2004. https://mudcat.org/thread.cfm?threadid=74275.
2. Neil Katz. "Life-size Barbie's shocking dimensions (PHOTO): Would she be anorexic?" 2011. https://www.cbsnews.com/news/life-size-barbies-shocking-dimensions-photo-would-she-be-anorexic/.
3. Nikolay Lamm. "What Would Barbie Look Like as An Average Woman?" 2013. https://nickolaylamm.com/.
4. Neil Katz. "Life-size Barbie's shocking dimensions (PHOTO): Would she be anorexic?"
5. The Wellness Institute. "The New Trim-Life® "What Are You Really Hungry For?" (An Exclusive Program of the Wellness Institute.) 1, 62.
6. The New Trim-Life® "What Are You Really Hungry For?"
7. Johnston. *Eating in the Light of the Moon.* 14.
8. Mudcat Café, "Hanna, My Delta Gamma" thread. Accessed April, 2025. https://mudcat.org/detail_pf.cfm?messages__Message_ID=1294071.
9. National Eating Disorders Association. "Statistics." Accessed

April 2025. https://www.nationaleatingdisorders.org/statistics/#general-eating-disorder-statisticsnot.

CHAPTER 7
DUST BUNNIES AND MY KITCHEN SINK

I have a clean kitchen sink. Since I really love clean smells, I wipe my sink with paper towels soaked in Pine Sol throughout the day. My kitchen floor is always spotless, too. I've wondered if little pieces of rice, crumbs, or a variety of dust bunnies distract me because I'm retired and hang out at home a lot. Boredom doesn't appear to be the trigger prompting my obsessive-compulsive behavior either. I'm enjoying one of the happiest and most productive times of my life.

Following retirement as an academic superintendent from a large urban school district, I became certified as a heart-centered hypnotherapist, transpersonal hypnotherapist, Reiki master, and energy healer. I study comprehensive energy psychology, meta-physics, trauma, and addictions. I'm blessed with an awesome family and a beloved community of friends. Thirteen years ago, I launched Educational Alchemist, LLC, offering workshops, coaching, consult-ing, and individual healing sessions. My work involves integrating leadership, equity, wellbeing, and consciousness. I'm living my dream! I have a clean kitchen sink.

In late Fall 2017, while teaching an online graduate diversity course, I noticed that my startle response was being triggered between seventeen and twenty times a day. Siri startles me when she hasn't given me driving directions for several miles. Emergency sirens make me jump out of my skin. My body jerks when I am startled by certain notes while listening to music, and any loud, unexpected noise makes my heart skip several beats. I understand that my nervous system responds to these noises in the same way it would if I were to come face-to-face with a tiger, need to lift a car off my grandchild, or jump out of a burning building. I am not experiencing tigers, cars, or fires, yet blood flows from my brain to my limbs, preparing me to take the life-saving actions of fight, flight, or freeze. Cortisol and adrenaline course through my body.

Intellectually, I understand that unconsciously, I'm being hyper-vigilant. I know that this takes a toll on my body. I understand on some rational level that picking up crumbs and scrubbing my sink are behaviors that distract me from feeling painful emotions like anxiety, fear, and shame. These cleaning activities could be ways my body is attempting to get rid of excess energy that was never used to fight or flee from traumatic events. Unconsciously, I am trying to regulate my nervous system by taking action (cleaning my sink) that moves me from being frozen to a state of sympathetic activation. This experience and others that I'm including in my story, have helped me come to know, love, and appreciate my body. The miracle of our mind-body connection is at the heart of my story, and why I believe so passionately that it's a story worth sharing.

During the holidays that year, I was diagnosed with complex PTSD. The startle response I experience comes directly and unconsciously from my body. It is not something I think about and execute. It's my body's signal to pay attention. My reptilian brain is wired for survival.

My journey through cognitive therapy led to incredible insights. My always-thinking, wise adult self was aware from years of experiencing hypnotherapy that not feeling safe in the world is a deeply seated, subconscious belief that I hold. Until this point, I hadn't been able to connect my present life with not feeling safe. I live alone, travel in areas devasted by urban decline and neglect, married and divorced twice as a means of caring for myself, traveled to South Africa shortly after 9/11, and consider myself a risk taker. I've walked on fire. I don't obsessively compulsively lock and recheck doors. One of my mantras is, I AM SAFE. I have a clean kitchen sink.

I am a White woman (this matters). My therapist was a beautiful, young (age is relative), Black (this matters) woman. During our initial in-take interview, she asked about my trauma history. In my typical, held together, I can always manage to look and sound good manner, I began to tell her my trauma story. The initial diagnosis was late-onset PTSD. My therapist and I set out on a twelve-week journey to the dark side of the moon and back. (This was the initial title for my book.)

During one of our weekly sessions, my therapist asked how I was feeling about my professional work experience with (trigger warning) "the angry Black woman" (not meant as a microaggression) who was terminated from her contract several months after a letter I had written to her was leaked to the press. (The therapist made a linguistic bridge by using my exact words from an earlier meeting). I explained (thinking head) that I was over it and that I had used hypnotherapy, breathwork, NET (neuro-emotional technique), acupuncture, polarity therapy, and meditation as alternative healing modalities to recover from my shocking, traumatic experience. I have no nightmares, flashbacks, or fears of people or places related to the trauma. My body is such an ally, an integrated part of my whole BE-ing, that I immediately started shaking, crying, numbing, getting choked up, and talking fast. I quickly became aware that I was not only out of coherence (heart and brain in alignment), but I was also experiencing parasympathetic and sympathetic shock at the same time. My body doesn't lie. My body is aware of things my mind simply can't wrap its brain around! Here is what my body had been holding on to for more than ten years. My kitchen sink is clean.

During the 2016 presidential campaign and subsequent election, there were numerous protests across the United States. Many of these protests were in response to rhetoric and policies that were perceived as racist and divisive. These events highlighted the deep divisions and tensions in the country, sparking a national conversation about racism, White supremacy, and the impact of political rhetoric. Black Lives Matter emerged as a global movement following the deaths of several young Black boys and men.

During the summer of 2017, White supremacists organized a Unite the Right Rally held in Charlottesville, Virginia. White supremacists marched through the city and carried burning torches as they walked the grounds of the historic and beautiful campus at the University of Virginia. They congregated in parks, surrounded statues, and made their way downtown. Their racist remarks echoed through the city streets. Protesters carried signs. Crowds gathered. A young woman was killed in the chaos.

Pictures of hooded figures, burning torches, protesters, flags, and crowds surrounding the victim flooded the media. Political rhetoric added fuel to the fire.

I am a White woman who left my home and family to take an assistant superintendent position in the Midwest in hopes of helping to close gaps in educational experiences and outcomes. Much of my career has been focused on equity, anti-racist education, and developing cultural competence. I brought valuable skills, knowledge, beliefs, and hope with me as I began my new position in the city schools. Things went downhill fast. I found myself in the middle of a toxic work environment. My integrity and values were challenged. A personal letter I had written to my boss was leaked to the press. I've come to know that the story and the details don't really matter and that recounting them only serves to give the experience more energy, but there is one piece that needs to be included. I sat in the front row along with colleagues during a televised board of education meeting. The head of a prominent community organization said, while looking at me (my memory), "It's time for you rednecks to take off your white hoods ... and it's time for the alleged whistleblower to be fired."

Tensions increased across the city. Undercover police attended school board meetings. Shortly thereafter, my boss was terminated. I was demoted and learned I didn't meet the legal requirements to qualify as a whistleblower. I used food for comfort. I gained weight. My husband and I separated. I suffered in silence.

For thirteen years, much of the fear, shock, and trauma related to this two-year period has been buried deep in my body. Unconsciously, my body remained in hyper-vigilant mode. My reptilian brain sent messages throughout my system: DANGER, DANGER, DANGER. All the energy I automatically mustered to respond to this perceived threat by fighting, fleeing, or freezing never saw the light of day. I've been carrying this weight around for an exceptionally long time. Seeing the pictures of White supremacists wearing white hoods and carrying torches through Charlottesville that summer, while I was teaching a diversity course, was enough to trigger the trauma and to bring this experience up for greater healing. My body holds the memory that's too painful to bear.

Throughout my life, I've experienced a great deal of trauma and shock. The thing about shock is that one can experience shock and not be aware of it! As you've seen, releasing shock is related to my healing voyage through PTSD.

"And the moon said to me—my darling daughter, you do not have to be
whole in order to shine."
-Nichole McElhaney

REFLECTIONS

"The greatest thing then, in all education, is to make our nervous system our ally as opposed to our enemy."
–William James

Polyvagal Theory

Earlier in my story, I mentioned that it's possible for all mammals to spoon when they feel safe and connected. Polyvagal theory is all about safety and connection, and by now, I'm certain that my responses of overwhelm around food and fear of hunger originated because I did not feel safe and I did not feel connected. According to author C.J. Llewelyn, the vagus nerve is a powerful nerve bundle that connects the brain to various organs, including the heart, lungs, and digestive system.[1]

Polyvagal theory is a fascinating concept developed by Dr. Stephen Porges.[2] It explains how our nervous system, specifically the vagus nerve, influences our emotional and physiological responses. According to the theory, our autonomic nervous system operates in three different states and is supported by several foundational concepts.

Ventral Vagal State: This is the state of safety and social engagement. When we're in this state, we feel calm, connected, and able to engage with others.

Sympathetic State: This is the state of fight or flight. When we're in this state, our body is preparing to either confront or escape from a perceived threat.

Dorsal Vagal State: This is the state of shutdown or immobilization. When we're in this state, we may feel numb, disconnected, or unable to respond to the environment around us.

Neuroception: This is the process by which our nervous system constantly scans for safety or danger without our conscious awareness. Deb Dana describes it like a built-in radar that helps us decide which state to enter.[3]

Hierarchy: These states are organized in a hierarchical manner. Dana walks us through the hierarchy. We first try to stay in the ventral vagal state, but if we perceive danger, we move to the sympathetic state. If the threat persists and we feel overwhelmed, we may shift to the dorsal vagal state.[4] When they spoon, mammals are in the highest state, ventral vagal.

Co-regulation: This is a key concept emphasizing our biological need to connect with others to create a shared sense of safety. This involves the reciprocal sending and receiving of signals of safety between individuals. This can happen through facial expressions, vocalizations, touch, and other forms of nonverbal communication. Dana writes that the concept of co-regulation starts from infancy, "where caregivers and infants engage through facial expressions, vocalizations, and touch, fostering a sense of safety and attachment."[5]

When I learned about co-regulation, I began to wonder how being in an incubator impacted my sense of safety and connection shortly after my birth. Was I attempting to engage with a fan in hopes of being comforted by touch, facial expressions, and sounds?

Premature babies, especially those born extremely preterm, can face a range of long-term challenges that may contribute to feelings of chronic emptiness or emotional struggles later in life. Chronic emptiness is a persistent feeling of numbness, disconnection, and lack of fulfillment. I'm wondering if chronic emptiness due to the loss of my twin is the source of the beliefs that I took on in utero: *I'm not safe; I might die; there is never enough; it's my fault, and I AM HUNGRY*.

Polyvagal Theory and Eating Disorders

Disordered eating and chronic emptiness are often connected, especially in individuals with underlying emotional or psychological issues. Individuals may turn to disordered eating to cope with feelings of emptiness and emotional pain.

Food can become a source of comfort or a way to fill the emotional void. In this way, disordered eating serves as a coping mechanism. Disordered eating behaviors can be a misguided attempt to manage overwhelming emotions and achieve a sense of control. Here, disordered eating serves as emotional regulation. People with chronic emptiness might struggle with low self-worth and use food to punish themselves or cope with a negative self-image. In this case, overwhelming emotions related to self-worth manifest as disordered eating.

In the context of eating disorders, polyvagal theory suggests that disordered eating behaviors may be a way to regulate the autonomic state and seek safety. "For instance, when someone feels unsafe or overwhelmed (sympathetic state), they might turn to food for comfort or control (dorsal vagal state). This can lead to patterns like binge eating or restrictive eating as coping mechanisms."

Author and blogger Isa Robinson, writes that, "In sympathetic activation state, eating disorders can show up through obsessive thoughts about food and food rituals, loss of appetite, binge eating, irritable bowel syndrome symptoms or excessive exercise (examples of the flight response). The fight response can be observed in the eating disorder symptoms of purging, chewing, and spitting, anger turned toward the body and other self-harm behaviors."[6]

Furthermore, "The dorsal vagal shutdown or the freeze response presents itself in eating disorders through inhibition in digestion, irritable bowel syndrome, desire to disappear, and use of extreme measures to feel the body such as extreme sports." [7]

Understanding these states and how they influence behavior can be crucial for treatment. By recognizing triggers and learning to regulate the nervous system through mindfulness and other techniques, individuals can work towards a more balanced and healthy relationship with food.[8]

Sitting with friends, eating dinner with my hands in the green beans, I was in a state of dorsal vagal activation. We can tell from the picture that I was spacing out. My boyfriend was a server in the kitchen. By then, I was restricting in hopes of being relished by the best of men. Smoking and swimming were my body's ways of moving up from vagal activation to a state of sympathetic activation.

While teaching the nuns that sunny morning, my body was numb, and I felt myself shutting down. I was experiencing dorsal vagal activation. Without knowing it, my choice to get a drink of water helped me to move up to the state of sympathetic activation. The act of walking out of the room and drinking something cold was my body's attempt to take flight.

As I sit and draft my story, I feel safe, sociable, and engaged. I'm waking up early. I'm attempting to see and write about the big picture of making peace with food and hunger. I can rest and digest, which are signs of a healthy parasympathetic state of being.

It's my sense that I've spent much of my life moving between parasympathetic and sympathetic shock, moving between being mobilized and shutting down. In some ways, life's been a dance between overdoing and underbeing!

I once described myself as the Energizer Bunny. My typical speed was on. That looks like overdoing, overthinking, overworking, talking fast, walking fast, and being happy all the time. These are signs of sympathetic shock. Unexamined and unexpressed painful emotions were my stuffing. Stuffing weighed me down. I'd disassociate from uncomfortable feelings by trancing out on TV, mindlessly scrolling social media, eating, and feeling powerless. These are signs of parasympathetic dissociation.

Polyvagal theory helps us understand how our bodies and minds are interconnected and how we can better manage our stress and emotions by recognizing which state we're in and finding ways to move back to a state of safety and connection. I've been learning to recognize what autonomic nervous system state is activated at various times throughout my day. With practice, I'm learning to transition from states of heightened arousal or shutdown to a state of calm, connection, and safety. Incorporating music and vagus nerve stimulation has helped me regulate my nervous system.

"The vagus nerve serves as the unlocked gate to your inner peace. If you understand spirituality as a connection to the Soul Self within you, and how this Soul Self is experiencing being human, your nervous system is the pathway to staying connected to your peace." [10]
-C.J. Llewelyn

NOTES

1. Llewelyn. *Chakras and the Vagus Nerve*. xviii.

2. Stephen W. Porges. "Polyvagal Theory: A Science of Safety." 2022. https://pubmed.ncbi.nlm.nih.gov/.

3. Deb Dana. *The Polyvagal Theory in Therapy: Engaging the Rhythm of Regulation*. (New York. W.W. Norton & Company, Inc., 2018) 4.

4. Dana. *The Polyvagal Theory in Therapy*. 32.

5. Dana. *The Polyvagal Theory in Therapy*. 44-47.

6. Isa Robenson. "Polyvagal Theory, Disordered Eating & Eating Disorders." 2021. https://isarobinsonnutrition.co.uk/blog.

7. Robenson. "Polyvagal Theory, Disordered Eating & Eating Disorders."

8. Unyte. ILS Integrated Listening Systems. Safe & Sound Protocol Training. (Littleton, CO, 2021).

9. Touch Therapy Tech for Stress Relief. https://apolloneuro.com/.

10. Llewelyn. *Chakras and the Vagus Nerve*. 2.

CHAPTER 8
MY BRAIN LOOKS LIKE A CHRISTMAS TREE

A few childhood memories came up as I began to write this next section. I was sitting in the back seat of my mother's car with my siblings in a grocery store parking lot. Mom hadn't come out of the store yet. A strange man opened my brother's car door and started to lean in. I leapt out of my side of the car as fast as a six-year-old could. It turns out the strange man was a teenager carrying my mother's groceries, and he was simply trying to put the bags in the car.

We moved when I was about six. I remember standing in the kitchen of our old house and asking my mom if we were the good guys or the bad guys. That's big thinking for a kindergartener. For several nights, shortly after our move to the new house, I'd wander out of my bed and tiptoe to my parents' room to make sure they were there. I recognize that all three memories are related to safety.

My intuition, or heart's wisdom, is as strong as my kitchen sink is clean. My gut told me that taking money from my retirement savings to have brain scans done at the Amen Clinic was an important part of my healing and teaching journey. In February 2018, following two days of PET scans, I was able to see pictures of my brain! Compared to healthy brain scans, my brain looks like a Christmas tree. The hopeful news is that there is good activity in my cerebellum.

A basic understanding of the brain will be helpful before I share details about where my brain lights shine. The brain is divided into three major structures: the brain stem, the limbic system, and the cortex. The brain develops in a hierarchical progression starting with simple functions and moving to more complex processes.

Brain Stem: Often called the reptilian brain due to its primal functions, the brain stem controls basic life-sustaining functions like heart rate, breathing, and sleep. It's the oldest part of the brain, evolutionarily speaking.

Limbic System: This is sometimes called the emotional brain. It includes structures like the amygdala and hippocampus, which are crucial for emotions, memory, and our sense of smell. The limbic system drives our primal emotions and behaviors, such as fear, pleasure, and anger.

Cortex: Also known as the neocortex or higher reasoning brain, this area is involved in complex functions such as perception, thought, problem-solving, and planning. It's the most recently evolved part of the brain and allows for higher-order thinking, language, and consciousness.

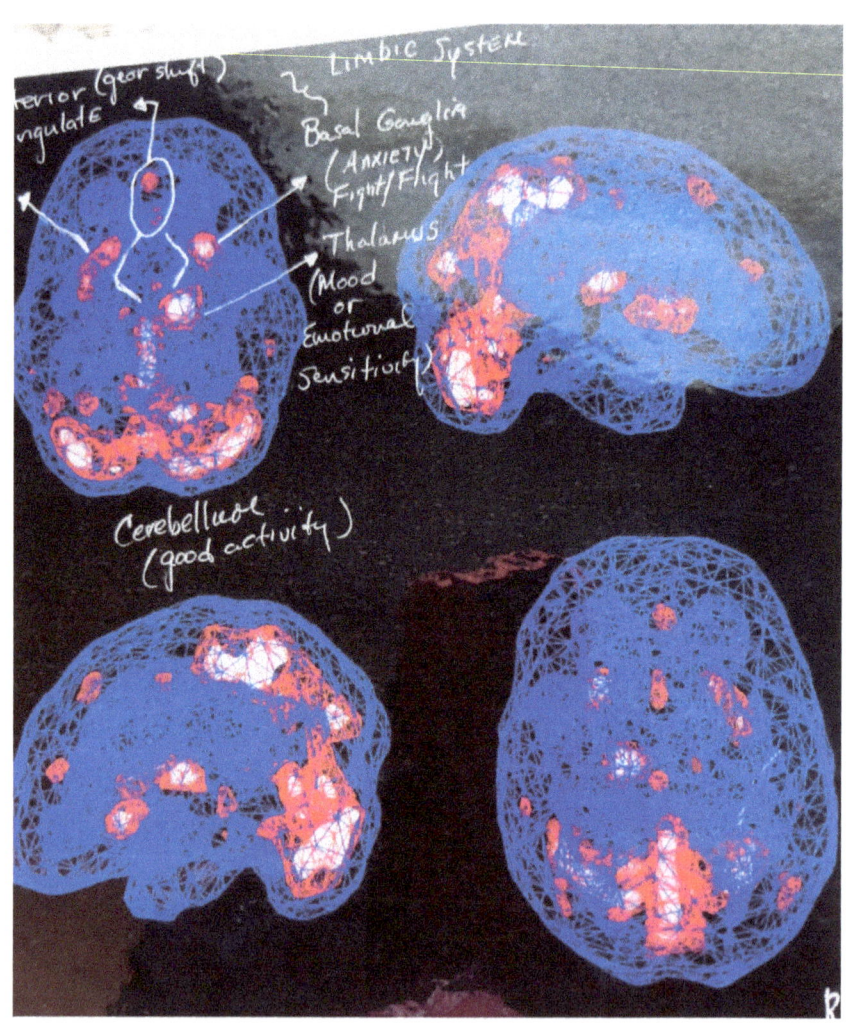

My SPECT Findings (1/23/18) Recorded in Amen Clinic Patient Record

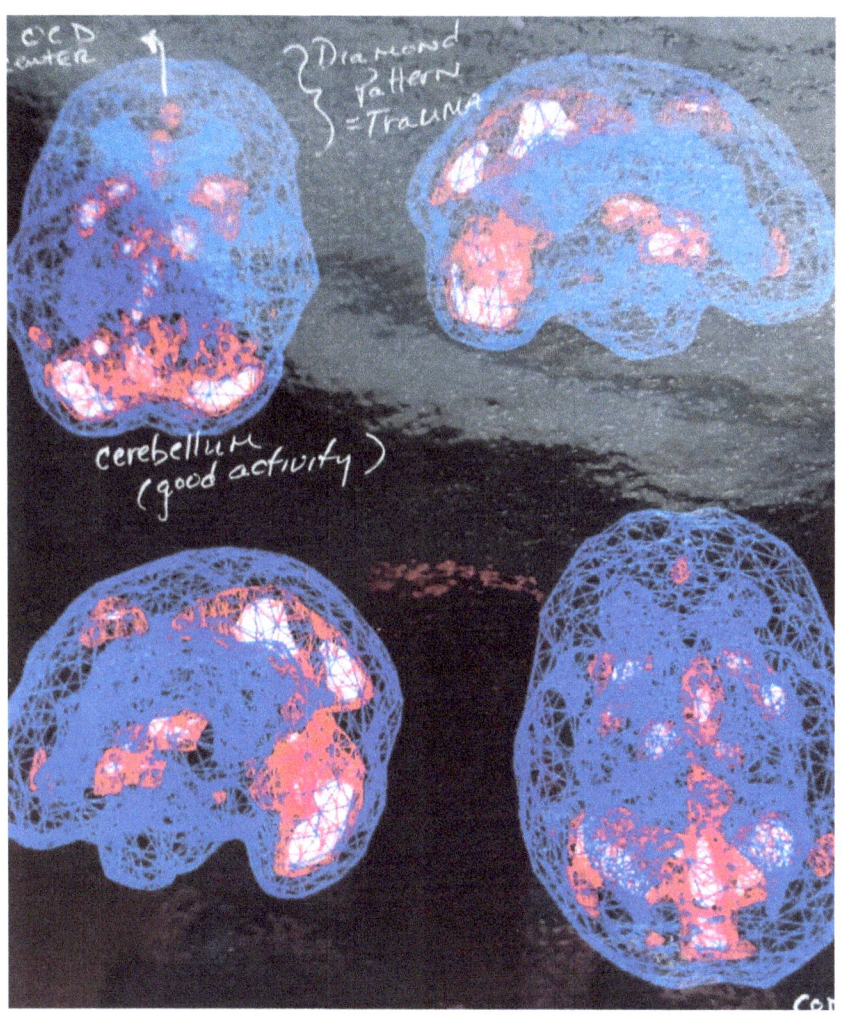

My SPECT Findings (1/23/18) Recorded in Amen Clinic Patient Record

Experts at the Amen Clinic assert that, "Brain SPECT imaging shows us three things: areas of the brain that work well, areas of the brain that work too hard, and areas of the brain that do not work hard enough."[1] Below are the significant findings from my scans, according to my patient records from the Amen Clinic.

"Low blood flow to temporal lobes can correlate with memory loss, anxiety, and irritability. Mild drop of blood flow to prefrontal cortex affects focus, concentration, executive function, and impulse control. Good cerebellar activity. The cerebellum coordinates movement and balance as well as thought coordination. There is a diamond pattern of activity which correlates with an emotional trauma history. Basal ganglia are overactive, which regulate fight or flight and will contribute to your physical anxiety manifestations. Your anterior cingulate is overactive which correlates with obsessive/compulsive thoughts and behaviors such as binging. Calming the limbic area will help with mood and anxiety. Findings are suggestive of a history of brain injury. Diagnosis: PTSD, chronic; generalized anxiety disorder; OCD (obsessive compulsive disorder); BED (binge eating disorder)."[2]

My brain looks like a Christmas tree. I have a clean kitchen sink. I may always need to engage in practices to calm my limbic system, which regulates mood and anxiety. I've found the practices listed below helpful in this pursuit.

Mindfulness and Meditation: Practicing mindfulness and meditation can help reduce stress and increase emotional regulation. Techniques like deep breathing, guided imagery, or mindfulness exercises can be beneficial.

Physical Activity: Regular exercise can reduce anxiety and stress by releasing endorphins, which help improve mood and emotional wellbeing. I typically swim four days a week.

Healthy Diet: Eating a balanced diet rich in omega-3 fatty acids, antioxidants, and other nutrients can support brain health and reduce stress. As you can tell, I'm working on this! I am practicing intuitive eating and avoiding any type of rigid dieting. I use the My Fitness Pal app most days as a guideline to pay attention to the nutrients I'm taking in to support brain health and reduce stress.

Adequate Sleep: Ensuring I get enough restful sleep is crucial for emotional regulation and overall brain health. Establishing a regular sleep routine can help. I wear a CPAP for sleep apnea, which I hope is a temporary intervention! Fortunately, I've always slept well.

Social Connections: Maintaining strong social bonds and seeking support from friends and family can help reduce stress and improve emotional wellbeing. I have wonderful social connections. Many people believe that connections are key to healing addictions. As you've already read, safety and connection are critical to our survival.

Relaxation Techniques: Practices like yoga, tai chi, and progressive muscle relaxation can help reduce stress and promote relaxation. Swimming and quiet time over coffee in the morning are my preferred ways to relax. I spend at least an hour every morning sitting quietly in my pajamas, drinking coffee, and just BE-ing. I've done this for more than thirty years.

Therapy and Counseling: Seeking professional help from a therapist or counselor can provide strategies and support for managing stress and emotional regulation. I've done it all! Hypnotherapy, breathwork, EFT (Emotional Freedom Technique or tapping), EMDR (Eye Movement Desensitization and Reprocessing), CBT (Cognitive Behavioral Therapy), and core energetics, which is a comprehensive approach to therapy that integrates body, mind, and spirit to promote healing and personal growth.

Hobbies: Activities I enjoy can provide a sense of fulfillment and relaxation, helping to calm the limbic system. My inner artist is emerging. I enjoy acrylic painting and am beginning to practice neurographic art. This therapeutic form of art encourages the brain to create new neural pathways and connections, aiding in emotional healing and self-discovery.

I am passionate about stamping out the stigma that is often associated with mental illness. At this point in my life, I'm embracing my vulnerability and sharing my story in hopes that it will be helpful to others on their healing journeys.

Before I move on to my reflections, it's important for me to acknowledge that the therapy I've had and the practices I use to calm my limbic system involve time and money. It's hard for me to imagine doing this when I was working full-time and raising children on my own. It also takes planning and making choices to sustain some of these practices on a limited retirement budget. I am fortunate to have benefits that cover some appointments and prescriptions. Unfortunately, many alternative healing modalities like hypnotherapy, breathwork, massage, Reiki, functional medicine, cranial sacral therapy, acupuncture, and others are not covered in most insurance plans, or they require a medical or mental health diagnosis.

I choose to be part of movements that support employee mental health and wellbeing, social-emotional development for youth and for adults in the workplace, heart-centered leadership, conscious parenting, and efforts like the surgeon general's framework for workplace mental health and wellbeing. [3] The plan, released in 2022, focuses on five key essentials. [4]

Protection from Harm: Ensuring physical and psychological safety by reducing workplace hazards and promoting a safe environment.

Connection and Community: Fostering a sense of belonging and social support among employees.

Work-Life Harmony: Supporting employees in balancing their work responsibilities with personal life.

Mattering at Work: Helping employees feel valued and recognized for their contributions.

Opportunity for Growth: Providing opportunities for professional development and career advancement.

Surgeon General 2022[5]

REFLECTIONS

As of this writing (Fall 2024), the only PTSD symptom that I'm aware of is an occasional startle response. I take medication to manage anxiety. I'm not aware of any traumatic injuries to my head, so I don't stew over that finding. The other SPECT results aren't surprising.

As I went back through the charts that describe birth issues for twins, premature babies, antiseptic birth, post-partum separation, and drugs (in my mother's case, possibly tobacco and alcohol), I found several issues worth exploring in the context of my brain scans. After all, I opened my story by saying, "So, recovery from disordered eating is really a spiritual path. Since we are spiritual beings in human bodies, recovery from disordered eating is also a neurobiological healing journey."

Are any of these conditions related to the SPECT scans? Are any of these conditions related to the pain I still carry about food and hunger?

Codependency

"Codependency is a behavioral condition in relationships where one person enables another's addiction, poor mental health, immaturity, irresponsibility, or underachievement. It often involves excessive emotional or psychological reliance on a partner, particularly one who requires support due to illness or addiction. Codependency can develop from dysfunctional family dynamics and childhood experiences where an individual learns to prioritize the needs of others over their own to gain acceptance or avoid rejection."[6]

It took me a while to really get the hang of what it means to be codependent. I'm aware of engaging in several codependent relationships, and I'm likely to discover more. I've learned that codependency was at the center of a longtime friendship based on trauma at work. I prioritized the needs of others in both marriages to gain acceptance or avoid rejection. This is codependent behavior. I enabled a work colleague by not challenging her pattern of irresponsibility. I'm still discerning patterns of codependent behavior that stem from family dynamics and childhood experiences. One that comes to mind is that my mom, one brother, sister, and I all hid the fact that we were all sneaking off to smoke. We each pretended we didn't know the family was full of smokers. As I reflect on my experience of sexual abuse at a young age and my choice not to tell my parents, I get a glimpse of the dance that characterizes codependent relationships. I was the codependent pleaser or fixer, the one who knew not to rock the boat by sharing this news. On some level, my young brain grasped the concept of unintended consequences. One or both of my parents may have been the controller or taker. They may have unconsciously sent the message that there is no room for drama here.

Addiction

Addiction is a complex condition characterized by compulsive behavior despite negative consequences. It's not just about substances like drugs or alcohol; behaviors such as gambling, eating, or using the internet can also be addictive. Gabor Maté asserts that addictions can be traced back to traumatic events during childhood. [7]

I'm owning up to my addictions. My quest to heal struggles with eating, and the cognitive dissonance between my behavior and my knowing who I am at my core became unbearable. I'm aware that I use TV and internet scrolling as ways to get dopamine or a feel-good rush. Awareness is the first step.

"When you find an addiction, do not be ashamed. Be joyful. You have found something that you have come to this earth to heal. When you confront and heal an addiction, you are doing the deepest spiritual work that you can do on this earth."
-Gary Zukov

Powerlessness

Powerlessness is a state of feeling unable to influence or control events and circumstances in one's life. This feeling can be pervasive and deeply unsettling, often leading to frustration, despair, and a sense of being trapped. In the context of addiction and recovery, recognizing powerlessness is an essential step toward healing. Elizabeth Van Sickel advises mental health practitioners that understanding powerlessness can lead to a more profound sense of humility and openness, creating space for growth, healing, and the development of healthier coping mechanisms.[8]

As most babies do, I felt powerless. This was exacerbated by being in the incubator. I missed touch, the sounds of my mother's voice, and being rocked when I was in distress. At an unconscious level, I felt powerless when I was sexually abused. There is a significant connection between sexual abuse and the development of eating disorders. Survivors of sexual abuse often experience intense feelings of shame, guilt, and a need for control, which can manifest in disordered eating behaviors.

As an adult, much of my anxiety related to food and hunger is an overwhelming feeling of powerlessness.

Looks to material objects for emotional support

Thomas Henricks helps us understand how physical things facilitate connection and support identity development. When a person derives emotional support and comfort from material things, this is referred to as emotional attachment to objects or transitional objects. These items can provide a sense of security, stability, and emotional connection, especially during times of stress or change. "In psychology, this concept is discussed in the context of transitional objects for children, such as a favorite blanket or stuffed animal. For adults, similar attachments can develop to objects that hold sentimental value or symbolize important relationships or memories."[9]

As a child, I had a slew of beloved stuffed animals. I treated them like friends that had feelings and could feel happiness or pain. I had a crushing sense of empathy and sympathy for the Trix Rabbit. I felt his pain. Trix Cereal was for kids, not rabbits! I'm a Taurus, and it's said that we love and appreciate all things beautiful and delicious. This resonates. I love my home—the colors, fabrics, furniture, and art. As you already know, I'm also called to taste and enjoy delectable foods.

Dissociation, numb

Dissociation is a mental process where a person disconnects from their thoughts, feelings, memories, or sense of identity. It's often a response to trauma or extreme stress.[10] Emotional numbness is a state where you may feel disconnected from your emotions or feel flat and detached.

I hadn't given much thought to the notion of dissociation or emotional numbness until I began my hypnotherapy training. I recognize both states of being, which you'll recognize throughout my story. Eating has been a common means of disconnecting from painful thoughts and emotions.

Longing to be overly connected to the spirit world

Pre and perinatal expert Annie Brook finds that "the longing to connect with the spirit world, particularly with animals like dolphins and whales, is a deeply rooted feeling for many people. Dolphins and whales are often seen as symbols of wisdom, peace, and connection to the natural world and the spiritual realm."[11]

Spiritual bypass is the only way I can think of to "be overly connected" to the spirit world. This refers to the tendency to use spiritual beliefs or practices to avoid facing unresolved emotional issues or psychological wounds.[12] My third-grade year impacted me on many levels. I wanted to be a nun and dressed in a costume given to me by my grandmother. I wanted a daily missal for my ninth birthday, complete with ribbons and colored pictures. I went to early mass each weekday morning. In doing so, I was allowed to eat my breakfast at school. It's possible that I was motivated by carrying my barn lunch box with a silo thermos and having the privilege of eating in my classroom! During this time, I was chosen to kiss the bishop's ring during a confirmation ceremony.

I felt a stirring inside that I couldn't name. I perceived that my soul was a dinner plate above my stomach; my soul was where all the grace I received landed. Grace is what feeds the soul! I had a deep sense that I was connected to God. As I got older, I was physically, emotionally, and spiritually moved to "get saved" in several churches. Upon reflection, I have always felt a longing for connection to what I now call Spirit. I believe this stirring and longing for connection are at the heart of my call to adventure and the unbearable disconnect between my inside and my outside.

Based on my lived experiences and evidence of trauma history, my training, and the interpretation of my brain scans, I have a much better understanding of how and why codependency, addiction, powerlessness, connection with material objects, and dissociation are all rooted in my strong will to survive.

The purpose of my quest centers around healing trauma, regulating my nervous system, and making new neural connections that reinforce healthy, life-giving behaviors. My lifelong journey to deepen my spiritual connection has made it possible for me to hear my soul's calling and follow the wisdom of my heart.

"When we experience shame, we are often thrown into crisis mode ...

In this mode, the neocortex is bypassed and our access to advanced, rational, calm thinking and processing of emotion all but disappears ... we find ourselves becoming aggressive, wanting to run and hide and feeling paralyzed ..."
-Brené Brown

NOTES

1. https://www.amenclinics.com/.

2. https://www.amenclinics.com/.

3. Health and Human Services Wellbeing Resources. "Mental Health and Wellbeing in the Workplace." 2022. https://www.hhs. gov/surgeongeneral/reports-and-publications/workplace-well-being/ index.html.

4. Health and Human Services Wellbeing Resources. "Mental Health and Wellbeing in the Workplace."

5. Health and Human Services Wellbeing Resources. "Mental Health and Wellbeing in the Workplace."

6. Jeremy Sutton. "What is Codependency? 20 Signs and Symptoms." 2024. https://positivepsychology.com/codependency-definition-signs-worksheets/.

7. https://drgabormate.com/addiction/.

8. Elizabeth Van Sickel. "Facing Your Powerlessness in Addiction." 2020. https://www.restoredhopecounselingservices.com/.

9. Thomas Henricks. "Personality Props: Material Objects and the Self." 2022. https://www.psychologytoday.com/us/blog/the-path

ways-of-experience/202201/personality-props-material-objects-and-the-self?msockid=odef2dbe3cc56d3e0b253c053dd76c7d.

10. Mayo Clinic. "Dissociative Disorders" https://www.mayoclinic.org/diseases-conditions/dissociative-disorders/symptoms-causes/syc-20355215.

11. Brook. Birth's Hidden Legacy. 41.

12. Diana Raab. "The Empowerment Diary Spirituality What Is Spiritual Bypassing?" 2024   https://www.psychologytoday.com/us/blog/the-empowerment-diary/201901/what-is-spiritual-bypassing.

CHAPTER 9
ADVERSE CHILDHOOD EXPERIENCES (ACES)

Ididn't know about Adverse Childhood Experiences until I began hypnotherapy training. This was a surprise, having spent more than three decades supporting children in schools, many of whom have experienced abuse, neglect, mental health challenges, or violence in the home.

The CDC-Kaiser Permanente Adverse Childhood Experiences (ACE) study is one of the largest investigations of childhood abuse and neglect, household challenges, and later-life health and wellbeing. Toxic stress experienced in early childhood, referred to as ACEs, has been linked to chronic health problems, mental illness, and substance abuse in adulthood. Findings suggest ACEs are associated with childhood obesity. Girls may be more sensitive to obesity-related effects of ACEs than boys, sexual abuse has a greater impact on childhood obesity than other ACEs, and co-occurrence of multiple ACEs may be associated with greater childhood obesity risk.[1]

Here are some of the most common types of ACEs: [2]

Emotional abuse: An adult insults, puts down or swears at a child. An adult behaves in a way that makes the child afraid they will be hurt.

Physical abuse: An adult hits, kicks, or physically hurts a child.

Sexual abuse: An adult (or older child) touches a child in a sexual way, makes a child touch them in a sexual way, or has sex (or tries to have sex) with a child.

Violence in the home: A child sees adults in the home physically harming each other.

Substance use problems in the home: A household member has problems with drinking, drug use, or misusing prescription medicines.

Mental health problems in the home: A household member is depressed, has mental health issues, or has attempted or died by suicide.

Emotional neglect: An adult in the home doesn't make a child feel safe, protected, and cared for.

Physical neglect: An adult in the home doesn't make sure that a child's basic needs are met.

Other childhood experiences can cause trauma as well. For example, things like discrimination, being bullied, and being in foster care can also cause stress that may have long-term effects.

I took the Adverse Childhood Experiences Survey, adapted from https://acestoohigh.com/got-your-ace-score/.[3] A score of four or more (out of ten) increases one's risk of disease, social and emotional problems. My score was four. The significant effect of sexual abuse on obesity hit home with me.

ACEs are common. Approximately two-thirds of Americans have experienced at least one ACE and one in six have experienced four or more ACEs.[4] People who have multiple ACEs tend to have more physical and mental health problems than people with few or no ACEs. This may be because of physical changes that can happen in a child's body when they have ongoing stress. It may also be because of health-harming behaviors (like smoking or risky sexual behavior) that are more common in people with more ACEs.

Having had ACEs doesn't mean that you will have physical or mental health problems, it just means that your risk for those things is higher. There are things you can do to reduce the effects of ACEs and take care of your mental and physical health.

REFLECTIONS

A note of caution is important here. I've facilitated several workshops that included information about Adverse Childhood Experiences and in some cases offered the option to take a survey or similar questionnaire. Adults responded in diverse ways as they engaged with the material. I keep the following considerations in mind when teaching or coaching about ACEs.[5]

Emotional Distress: The survey can bring up painful memories and emotions, which might be distressing for respondents. It's important to provide a safe and supportive environment when conducting the survey.

Informed Consent: Ensure that respondents are fully informed about the purpose of the survey and the potential emotional impact it may have. They should have the option to opt out if they feel uncomfortable.

Confidentiality: Assure respondents that their responses will be kept confidential and used only for the intended purpose.

Professional Support: Have mental health professionals available to provide support if respondents experience significant distress during or after completing the survey.

Cultural Sensitivity: Be aware of cultural differences and how they might affect the interpretation of questions and responses.

Administering the ACE survey with these precautions can help mitigate potential harm and ensure that the information gathered is used ethically and effectively.

Sharing my story has been both a vulnerable and a healing experience. I believe that Trauma Informed Practice (TIP) in schools centers on a deficit model; a faulty belief that assumes children of color and from poverty are the (only) ones who experience trauma. As mentioned above, ACEs are common. This means that many people in schools, including adults, have experienced some sort of trauma. In sharing my story, I hope to diminish the stigma around mental health and trauma.

NOTES

1. Center for Child Counseling. "ACES Tool Kit." www.center forchildcounseling.org.

2. Center for Child Counseling. "ACES Tool Kit."

3. ACES Too High, LLC. "What ACES Do You Have." https://aces toohigh.com/got-your-ace-score/.

4. Center for Child Counseling. "ACES Tool Kit."

5. Center for Child Counseling. "ACES Tool Kit."

CHAPTER 10

DR. DEATH

L ike many of you, I've tried every diet on the planet, scoured the internet for quick fixes, and have spent too much money on books, groceries, and supplements. At one point, I began the process of qualifying for bariatric surgery. A good friend shared that he and his wife knew someone who died following this type of operation. He told me about Dr. Death.

Of course, Dr. Death was not his real name. We called him that because once you took his pills and injected the shots, you felt like you were dying for the first few days. I drove three hours to another state to have blood drawn, met with this physician, bought mystery pills, and drove home with a script for a weight loss drug. I did this periodically over a two-year period about fifteen years ago. I met Dr. Death long before Wegovy® and Ozempic® came on the scene.

For the first time in my life, I lost my appetite. Weight came off quickly. I lost forty-five pounds in three months. I kept the weight off for a while. My insurance changed. It no longer covered the daily injections. I gained back all the weight I had "lost."

One of the challenges I faced while using several different prescriptions was the onset of lichen sclerosis, an autoimmune condition that was confirmed following a biopsy. Several of the self-injection medicines listed side effects including bacterial infections that cause damage to the tissue under the skin, urinary tract infections, and yeast infections. To my knowledge, none cited a causal effect or relationship between the drug and lichen sclerosis.

Outbreaks are extremely painful. I've learned that eating some high-oxalate foods triggers these occurrences. Oxalates, also known as oxalic acid, are naturally occurring compounds in plants; you eat them in food, and your body produces them. Avoiding some of the healthiest foods I enjoy and learning which ones affect me contributes to the diet riot noise in my head. Although spinach is high in oxalates, I eat it without problems. Legumes are wonderful. Unfortunately, I can't eat most legumes and nuts. Green beans, okra, some teas, and kiwi contribute to outbreaks. At one point, desperate for answers, I was a card-carrying member of the Vulval Pain Society.[1]

REFLECTIONS

Let's talk about meds. Many of us would have never dreamed that we'd be introduced to life-saving drugs like Wegovy®, Ozempic®, and others in our lifetime. These drugs are helping many people release weight, decrease BMI, improve blood pressure, and experience numerous health benefits. For many of us, the cost of these prescriptions is prohibitive. Alternatives from compound pharmacies are also expensive and don't work for everyone, and many people gain weight when they stop the medication.

One lesson I'm learning on my journey is that we each must forge our own path. I believe that choosing to try new medications is a personal choice. Like walking on fire, discernment is key. With support from my primary care physician, I've recently chosen to try compounded tirzepatide. It's too early to tell if the drug is influencing my appetite, thoughts, behaviors, and slow but steady weight loss.

I know it is important to weigh the benefits and risks of medication and to make informed decisions about treatment options. Fortunately, I am more connected to my body and to my intuition than I was throughout treatment with Dr. Death. I rely on my heart's intuitive intelligence, discernment, and working in partnership with my healthcare practitioners to make wise decisions about my health.

Update Spring 2025: As I get ready to send the book to my editor, I want to share an update about my medication. My primary care physician facilitated the process of getting prior approval from my insurance company to cover part of the cost of Zepbound® (Tirzepatide). In addition to supporting patients with weight loss, this drug has been beneficial for patients like me who are treated for sleep apnea. I'm no longer taking the compounded tirzepatide injections.

NOTES

1. https://vulvalpainsociety.org/.

CHAPTER 11

WAITING FOR THE OTHER SHOE
TO DROP

Ninety-five percent of our behaviors are not conscious. Almost all our behavior patterns are driven by our subconscious or unconscious thoughts, feelings, emotions, and physiology. Only five percent of our behaviors in any given moment are driven by our conscious mind.

The Integrated Performance Model is a great tool for better understanding why we do what we do because so much of our behavior is driven by internal, invisible forces! Physiology matters.[1]

Integrated Performance Model

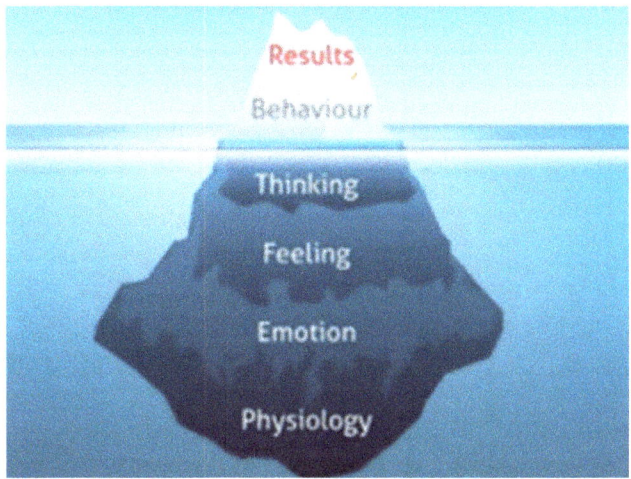

Coherence The Secret Science of Brilliant Leadership, Watkins, Alan. Reproduced with permission of the Licensor through PLSclear

Human performance expert Alan Watkins says, "What's really driving our behavior is our internal, invisible thinking. And what we think and how well we think it is largely determined by our internal and invisible feelings which are driven by our internal and invisible emotions which are made up of the myriads of internal and invisible biological physical signals and processes that make up our physiology at any given moment." [2]

I'm aware that most of our behaviors are not conscious. Since I pay attention to what is happening to me physically, emotionally, mentally, and spiritually, I'm able to walk you through an example of how this model works. Following retirement, I enjoyed consulting, teaching, and healing as the Educational Alchemist, LLC. One morning, I was sipping coffee in my pajamas, grateful that I typically never start work before 10:00 a.m. I was thinking about consulting work planned for the day and the stops I'd be making across the city. I noticed a tingling in my arms and prickling down my legs. This is awareness of my **physiology**, the internal biological signals represented at the bottom of the iceberg.

I've come to recognize these as signs of anxiety. Anxiety is an **emotion**—energy in motion. I stayed with the anxiety for a minute. Consciously moving up the iceberg, I noticed I was beginning to **feel** calm.

My body communicates with me. I began to talk to myself. My **thinking** went like this:

I recognize this tingling as anxiety. Hmmm. I'm not anxious about anything right now. I like my job and am excited to meet with people today.

I took a breath and focused on my heart center. I heard, *you're waiting for the other shoe to drop. Ahaa! Thank you, body. The other shoe isn't going to drop today. My job isn't dangerous anymore. I am safe. I'm not in charge. No need to be hyper-vigilant. You can relax now.*

Wait, there's more!

I wonder if my boss cares that I come in after 10:00 *a.m. He doesn't care. People are doing their jobs and are not wondering where you are or what you're doing. You're a consultant and aren't bound by a time clock. Maybe I charge too much money. Is my hourly rate too high? Am I worth what they are paying me? Does what I do add value? Am I good enough?"*

The most important part came next. I responded calmly to my thinking. I continued to talk to myself.

You are an impressive, talented human BE-ing who is great at DO-ing her job. I don't know anyone else who can lead schools and hypnotize people! My skill set is impressively unique, and I'm a sought-after heart-centered leader. I've healed so many wounds that I know in my heart I am good enough. I deserve to be paid fairly. We live in an abundant universe. I am safe.

I changed my thinking. This scenario didn't last more than a few minutes. I made a healthy choice to make my way up the iceberg. I chose to be conscious and connected to my body (**behavior**). I chose not to numb out by eating, procrastinating, mindlessly scrolling through social media, or isolating (**behavior**). I chose to feel my feelings and to change self-defeating thought forms. The **results** were my nervous system was regulated. I experienced pride, peace, and gratitude—emotions associated with resilience!

My biggest takeaway from experiencing and teaching the Integrated Performance Model is that **physiology matters**. The quest to thrive and achieve the results we seek begins in our bodies. We have a responsibility to learn to manage our energy. We must learn how to self-regulate without using food.

It's mind-blowing that ninety-five percent of our behaviors are unconscious. We struggle when we don't see the results we hope for. Most of us have no clue why we do what we do! The mind-body connection and practices like yoga, meditation, listening to music, guided visualization, art, and dance are ways that we make the unconscious conscious.

How we feel and what we think matters. A lot! Emotions and thoughts are energy. They are capable of depleting or renewing our energy reserves.

REFLECTIONS

In rereading this part of my heroine's journey, it strikes me that it's important to share that I no longer perseverate (a cool word that means "to repeat something, such as words or actions, over and over again.") about the patterns in my brain, the impact of starting life outside the womb in an incubator, my ACEs score, or the trauma responses that keep me in my head, disconnecting me from my heart, to avoid painful feelings like shame, fear, and powerlessness.

I know a good deal about powerlessness. Researching my dissertation, *Parent Participation and Alienation Among African American Mothers in Urban Schools: Effects of Involvement in Project Fast*, led me to an understanding of meaningless, normlessness, and powerlessness—all aspects of alienation. "Alienation occurs when a person withdraws or becomes isolated from their environment or from other people," writes Rachel Barclay on Healthline. "Powerlessness is believing that actions have no effect on outcomes or that you have no control over your life."[3]

I no longer feel powerless in my life. I feel powerful, strong, and vigorous. My thoughts, words, actions, and emotions impact my well-being. I am responsible for much of what happens in my life. I am not a victim. I am a teacher at heart and acknowledge that I've been merging some content within my stories and reflections. I've saved one of the best ones for last.

The Victim or Drama Triangle is a social model of human interaction. It maps out a type of destructive interaction that can occur among people in conflict. It's not a new concept, yet it's one that really helped me learn a lot about myself and to change my behavior. I've taught this model to more than one thousand educators and clients during the past fifteen years. Many have shared that learning to recognize when they take on the role of victim and how to change their behavior from reactive to responsive has been one of the most empowering life lessons they've experienced.

The triangle consists of three roles: persecutor, victim, and rescuer.

Persecutor: This person blames, criticizes, and is often controlling. They might say things like, "You never do anything right!"[4]

Victim: This person feels oppressed, helpless, and powerless. They often seek sympathy and validation from others, saying things like, "Poor me! I can't do anything right."[5]

Rescuer: This person tries to save the day, offering help and support, but often ends up enabling the victim. They might say, "Let me help you."[6]

The roles are fluid, and people can switch between them during interactions. The drama triangle can perpetuate negative feelings and behaviors, keeping individuals stuck in unhealthy patterns. It often prevents real change and resolution of underlying issues.

Recognizing these roles and understanding how they influence behavior is crucial for breaking the cycle. The good news is that we can get out of the victim/drama triangle. Awareness is the first step. With support, it's possible to learn new roles. For example, TED (the empowerment dynamic) introduces the healthy roles of creator, challenger, and coach.[7]

We typically talk about the roles in the context of relationships with others. We can also engage in all three roles by ourselves. Here's my personal diet example. I am playing all the roles in a one-woman drama!

Victim: *I hate this. There's a diet riot going on in my head, and I can't stop it. Everyone else loses weight on Keto. Men do not like curvy or overweight women. I hate my clothes. Why me?*

Rescuer: *I just found this new supplement that helps you lose five pounds overnight. I think you can also extend the hours that you are fasting overnight.*

Persecutor: *You blew it again by eating that piece of mincemeat pie and ice cream. Did you see the size of the portion you took? You're being careless with your money. The cupboards are full of supplements that work for everyone but you.*

As you've read by now, I've faced many challenges in life, just as you have. This is part of our human experience. Trauma survivors will enact all three roles at various times. We will follow these scripts because it feels essential to do so. These parts of the nervous system are linked to our survival mechanisms. Each drama triangle role is a product of the fight, flight, freeze, or fawn survival response experienced during trauma. Remember, awareness is the first step. When you find yourself reacting, pause and consider the role you are likely playing in the drama triangle!

Note of caution: Just because someone is in the victim role, it does not mean that their traumas and pains are invalid. Identifying as a victim in the drama triangle does not invalidate or diminish someone's traumatic experiences. Those experiences and feelings of suffering are real and valid.

NOTES

1. Alan Watkins. *Coherence: The Secret Science of Brilliant Leadership.* (London: Kogan Page, 2013) 3, 5.

2. Watkins Coherence: *The Secret Science of Brilliant Leadership.* 3, 5.

3. Rachel Barclay. "Understanding Alienation." 2024. https://www.healthline.com/health/alienation

4. The Attachment Project. "The Drama Triangle Explained." https://www.attachmentproject.com/psychology/drama-triangle/.

5. The Attachment Project. "The Drama Triangle Explained."

6. The Attachment Project. "The Drama Triangle Explained."

7. Center for the Empowerment Dynamic. https://theempowermentdynamic.com/.

SECTION TWO

HEADING HOME

HEADING HOME

This ends another phase of my heroine's journey framed as challenges. I've confronted enemies— souls who came into my life to trigger me so that I could learn valuable lessons. My inner critic contributed to much of the noise in my head. I acknowledged and integrated shadow parts of self.

I made allies along the way. Many of my allies have been gifted teachers, others incredible healers. Some have been students and colleagues, some part of my wellness and spiritual community, friends, and family. Many of these souls are acknowledged at the end of my story. My greatest ally is my wise adult self! She grows stronger every day.

I'm ready to pick up my metaphorical knapsack that now includes a diary of reflections made along my way. It's time to head home.

CHAPTER 12

LEGACY

Joseph Campbell's framework for the hero's journey includes a step known as resurrection when the hero faces a final challenge where everything is at stake. My final test lasted from August-December 2022.

I experienced a baffling, unidentified illness that shook me to my core. I had difficulty breathing, swallowing, eating, and coughing. The acid coming from my mouth caused damage to my vocal cords. I lost about thirty-five pounds and estimate that I was only eating between 500-800 calories most days. I drove myself to the ER four times. Since I live alone, I began sleeping on the living room couch with an overnight bag packed and the door unlocked so that the EMTs could enter my house. I met with every "ologist" one could imagine: rheumatologist, cardiologist, pulmonologist, gastroenterologist, and endocrinologist. I was incorrectly diagnosed with asthma, COPD, pneumonia, and GERD. I was prescribed harsh medicines that had no impact on my condition.

My fifth trip to the emergency room was by rescue squad. I was in atrial fibrillation during the intake with a new doctor. I was rear-ended by a small truck five days later. My car was totaled. Thankfully, other than adding more trauma to my already hyper-vigilant nervous system, I didn't sustain severe physical injuries. The experience was so debilitating and testing so invasive, that I began to wonder if I wanted to keep living. I've been taught that our soul may experience several choice points throughout a lifetime. We're being asked if we want to stay in our physical bodies or return to spirit form. My purpose is still unfolding, and I'm not yet finished with my work on this planet. I chose to stay.

There are several theories about the source of this illness, none confirmed. I no longer search for answers. I trust in my body and my innate ability to heal.

Having experienced the resurrection—this final test—I knew my transformation had taken place.

The Elixir

The heroine returns home transformed, often with a reward or newfound wisdom.

My personal mission is to bring light to this planet, helping people raise their levels of consciousness. I recognize that my own transformation is about so much more than making peace with food and hunger. My liberation (and yours, too) comes from a spiritual awakening that activates a permanent shift in consciousness, a recognition of one's true self, their divine nature, and the realization that the idea of separation from our original Source-God is an illusion. This shift in awareness is what I've been truly hungry for. In the beginning of my story, I wrote that recovery from disordered eating, and every other life challenge, is really a spiritual path. Since we are spiritual beings in human bodies, recovery from disordered eating is also a neurobiological healing journey.

I've come to understand that my heroine's journey has been about two paths toward wholeness and non-duality that we all travel—the **spiritual path,** and the **healing path**[1]. Both paths must be equally embraced and nurtured. A person who emphasizes the spiritual path by reading, praying, meditating, and practicing a religion, for example, but spends little energy nurturing the body or healing emotional issues is out of balance. Likewise, someone who emphasizes the healing path by doing yoga, breathwork, inner child work, and following nutritional laws while neglecting spiritual practices is also out of balance.[2] I chose to explore how traumatic events in my life impacted me physically, emotionally, mentally, and spiritually and to share healing modalities, concepts, and practices that have helped me along my journey to make peace with food and hunger. I hadn't been making a distinction between the two paths. It's clear through my stories, reflections, and experiences that I've been traveling both the spiritual and healing paths. It's possible that my anguish and soul's calling to write has been an attempt to bring balance to my journey by nurturing my spiritual growth.

In my storytelling, I've described heading out on my journey carrying an invisible knapsack filled with courage and grace. I wasn't aware I'd been carrying a map the whole time! Just as Dorothy never realized that her sparkly red shoes had the power to get her home at any point along her journey, my body (and yours as well) can be viewed as a map for exploring levels of consciousness that are relevant to the journey toward wholeness. Chakras are a wonderful entre into our psyche and physical wellbeing.

Chakras are the energy centers of the body. Each person has seven main chakras that correspond to bundles of nerves, major organs, and areas of our energetic body running from the base of the spine to the top of the head. When all our chakras are open, energy can run through them freely, and harmony can exist between our body, mind, and spirit. When a chakra is blocked, energy can get stuck and present itself as discomfort. Chakras parallel the emotional struggles we are working to heal. We have a chakra for each issue that we think about.

With awareness and practice, we can tell when our chakras are in balance, have excessive energy, or are depleted of vital life force energy. In this way, they can be viewed as a map or GPS on our spiritual and healing paths toward wholeness.

It's easy to find information on chakras. Materials and beliefs vary depending on the roots of those sharing a framework. Not intended to be exhaustive, here's one way to understand the seven chakras. I'm also sharing my reflections about connections between each chakra and the emotional struggles I'm healing.

Body-Root Chakra. Earth.
Safety, Security, Survival

The body-root or earth chakra relates to physical security, finances, career, home, needs, possessions, and masculine energy.

In balance: feelings of safety, security, and stability. You are grounded and connected to the physical world. You have confidence in your ability to meet life's challenges.

Out of balance: feelings of fear, insecurity, and instability. You may experience anxiety or physical issues like lower back pain.

Excessive: heavy body, slow, sluggish, attachment to security.

Deficient: scattered, ungrounded, spacey, flighty. Somatic experiences might include lack of energy, lethargy, lower back pain, leg tingling, and digestive issues.

Offers lessons of resilience, stability, renewal, and being present in the moment.

My physical initiations with the root-body chakra include wondering if I wanted to keep living during my mystery illness, using specific exercises to release trauma from my body, confounding physical looks and sexuality, and financial worries as a theme in my adult life. I also explored my hunger and became aware of leadership traits associated with the divine masculine, such as strength, action, confidence, rationality, authority, and responsibility. This caused me to reflect on the balance of masculine and feminine, head and heart. As a survivor of sexual abuse, my root chakra energy center was most likely distorted.

Several practices help me balance and cleanse my root chakra. Physical exercises like walking and swimming help me stay grounded. Meditations or guided visualizations help me focus on the base of my spine and the color red. I use positive affirmations such as, "I am safe and secure." My heroine's journey has helped me realize that I've continued to hold subconscious thoughts about not feeling safe in this world.

Emotion-Sacral Chakra. Water. Emotions, Creativity, Pleasure

The emotion chakra relates to cravings for physical pleasure, addictions, sexual energy, flexibility, feminine energy, emotional healing, and emotional safety.

In balance: fosters creativity and joy.

Out of balance: emotional instability and lack of inspiration.

Excessive: indulgent, over-emotional, sloppy, ill-intentioned promiscuity.

Deficient: rigid, dry, numb, flat emotions. Somatic experiences might include low libido, reproductive issues, low energy, lower back pain, and hormonal imbalances.

Offers lessons related to respecting one's body and caring for one's needs, exploring boundaries, and creating intimate relationships.

My emotional initiations are reflected throughout my journey and include the deep dive to explore traumas and share my experiences with various healing modalities. The process included surfacing awareness of the impact of shame and powerlessness in my life and my acknowledgment of illusions created in relationships. I have developed compassion for the part of me that connects betrayal with the loss of my twin and become aware of the spiritual and cultural concepts of the divine feminine that I embody, including empathy, intuition, creativity, collaboration, and nurturing. I am seeking to balance those with the divine masculine.

The sacral chakra is the center of our emotional and psychic selves. These aspects of growth are often associated with the subconscious. My experiences with hypnotherapy, inner child work, and counseling resulted in a great deal of emotional learning, processing, and getting in touch with my emotional and feminine nature. Themes of sensitivity, honesty, and vulnerability run through my story. I've shifted from states of utter powerlessness to much higher levels of emotional responsibility and self-regulation.

Several practices and new understandings help me balance and cleanse my sacral chakra. For example, I use guided visualizations and meditations where I connect with the color orange in my lower abdomen. I've often used affirmations such as, "I embrace change and nourish my soul."

Throughout my heroine's journey, I've often referred to emotions as energy in motion. Emotions can serve as a mirror of our healthy and unhealthy choices and beliefs. They reflect what we hold in our hearts and the kinds of experiences we are creating. We all feel both positive and negative emotions. Emotions are experienced on both the spiritual and healing paths.

Some of my most powerful lessons and experiences about emotions come from my HeartMath™ training and practices.[7] HeartMath™ frames these in an infographic that asks, did you know that negative emotions can create nervous system chaos, but positive emotions do the opposite? Positive emotions can increase the brain's ability to make good decisions. You can boost your immune system by focusing on positive emotions, which create physiological benefits in your body. Your heart emits an electromagnetic field that changes according to your emotions; others can pick up the quality of your emotions through the electromagnetic energy radiating from your heart.

The HeartMath™ Institute asserts that sustained positive emotions and heart-focused intentions can influence DNA conformation, potentially shifting physiological processes toward a state of coherence and optimal function.[4] The research suggests that generating feelings of love, appreciation, and compassion, combined with a specific intention, can influence DNA, potentially "winding" or "unwinding" DNA strands.

The concept of coherence (alignment of heart, brain, and nervous system) is introduced in an earlier section of my story. Here, it becomes clear how coherence relates to both our physical, emotional, mental, and intuitive (spiritual) consciousness. HeartMath™ research suggests that generating sustained positive emotions can lead to a state of psychophysiological coherence characterized by increased order and harmony in both psychological and physiological processes. The state of coherence is associated with greater emotional stability, increased mental clarity, and enhanced cognitive function.

I've taught and practiced HeartMath™ concepts, tools, and technologies for more than twelve years. This work has significantly influenced my spiritual and healing paths to wholeness.

Mind-Solar Plexus Chakra. Fire.
Personal Power, Control, Ego

The mind chakra relates to passion, the will to live, right action and core values, willpower, self-awareness, study, reason, logic, focus, organization, personal power, positive attitude.

In balance: self-confidence and motivation.

Out of balance: low self-esteem and indecision.

Excessive: controlling, dominating, bullying, constantly doing.

Deficient: weak, passive, victimized. Somatic experiences might include digestive issues, poor metabolism, increased metabolic rate, fatigue, and adrenal imbalances.

Offers lessons about one's unique purpose and power in the world, supports the evolution of the ego beyond the adolescent psyche, and can facilitate bringing one's soul into the world.

My mental initiations include recognizing the internal conflict I experience between willpower and control, healing unhealthy conclusions and thought forms like these:

> *There's never enough.*
> *I'll always be hungry.*
> *I'm going to die!*
> *Men never like women who carry extra weight.*
> *I'm not enough!*
> *I am powerless.*

I have become aware that my intellect is both a strength that serves me well at times, but at other times, it has been like an addiction, keeping me from feeling painful feelings.

115

Several practices and deeper understandings help me balance and cleanse my sacral chakra. I set personal goals and take on new challenges. Although I rarely practice yoga, I'm aware that the boat pose and warrior three can open the solar plexus. I frequently use affirmations such as *I am powerful,* and *I am confident.*

I used to describe myself as a walking, talking head and took pride in developing my intellect. The solar plexus chakra is commonly related to our intellectual self or lower mind (in contrast to the higher mind of the heart center). The solar plexus is a complex network of nerve fibers of the sympathetic nervous system. It both receives and transmits nerve impulses. Surprisingly, this center of the lower mind is associated with an emotion: fear. When we are in a state of fear, we go into thinking mode to try to escape (flight) the feeling of danger. Unconsciously, we call on the lower mind's help to handle the emotional discomfort. Our minds have limits as well as gifts. Many of us have experienced monkey mind, or the mind that just can't get quiet. Either spirit or ego can direct our minds. At times, we need to train the mind to focus and take action, and at other times to be left quiet to receive new insights, inspiration, heart wisdom, and connections to Source. I do healing work with individuals who want to develop physically, emotionally, mentally, and spiritually. Before I meet with clients, I have a ritual where I send my ego to a coffee shop so that it does not interfere with the session.

Mental consciousness develops as we awaken knowledge, focus, and determination—traits that many refer to as personal power. Thoughts actually manifest as things. It has taken me years to wrap my mind around this, but as I've experienced manifesting or creating my own reality, I've begun to pay attention to what I think. Positive thoughts create healthy manifestations, and negative thoughts create negative manifestations. The stronger the thought, the more powerful the results.

Heart Chakra. Air.
Relationships, Love, Attachments, Forgiveness/
Unforgiveness

The heart chakra relates to the balance of giving and receiving, code-pendency, compassion, divine love from God and the higher self, romantic, platonic, and familial love.

In balance: enables empathy and love.

Out of balance: can lead to feelings of bitterness, loneliness, unworthiness, and the inability to trust.

Excessive: co-dependent, meddlesome, needing attention.

Deficient: closed-hearted, judgmental, isolating. Somatic experiences may include poor circulation, high or low blood pressure, stiffness in the shoulders, chest, and upper back.

Offers lessons as one heals past wounds. It allows us to foster harmonious relationships with others, cultivate self-love, and balance giving and receiving.

My intuitive heart initiations include tapping into the artist and writer within, experiencing unconditional love for self and others, and recognizing the importance of returning to love when I find myself judging, comparing, and controlling. My capacity for forgiveness has grown exponentially, and I recognize that all the challenging experiences and people I attract have been opportunities for forgiveness, compassion, and unconditional love. I've learned that I was over-giving and under-receiving in many relationships. I've shared how I've been working to resolve past wounds throughout my story. I've experienced the "dark night of the soul" several times, having my life fall apart, questioning everything, and waking up with higher levels of consciousness. My divorce, nervous breakdown, work betrayals, disordered eating, and mystery illness all have served to crack my heart open and recognize my true self.

Several experiences, understandings, and practices help me balance and cleanse my heart chakra. I consciously practice acts of kindness, empathy, compassion, and patience. During meditation, I often place my hand on my heart and repeat affirmations such as, *I am love* and *I am open to love.* While breathing in, I often think to myself, *only love in.* While breathing out, I think *only love out.*

The heart chakra represents our intuitive and creative consciousness and opens us to our higher mind. I've been taught that this heart center is the symbolic home of the soul. Some describe this energy center as where heaven and earth meet. Here, we can make decisions guided by God or Source (located above and represented by the spiritual centers of consciousness in the neck and head), or by our lower self (the mind, emotions, and body). Motherhood is an initiation that awakened my heart to a much deeper level.

The mind learns by studying and thinking, while the heart learns by integrating experiences and feeling. My soul had been in anguish, and it's clear that I was moved to begin my quest at the invitation of my heart center. I was aware that my obsessions and compulsions about food and hunger were both driven by desires and impulses of the lower self, by a greater spiritual knowing that *it's not my fault,* and a call for purging and purifications. Attachment to worldly desires kept me from connecting to my true self and to God.

My heart wisdom has been about surrender, letting go, acceptance, and unconditional love.

"What is to give light must endure burning."
-Viktor Frankl

Throat Chakra. Ether.
Communication, Expression, Truth

The throat chakra refers to speaking your truth, communication projects (writing, speaking, singing, teaching), asking for your needs to be met by God, loved ones, employers, yourself, and creative expression.

In balance: express yourself clearly.

Out of balance: Shyness or difficulties in communication.

Excessive: loud, scattered, talks too much.

Deficient: fear of speaking. Somatic experiences can include neck stiffness, shoulder tension, teeth grinding, and jaw and throat ailments.

Offers lessons related to confidence and self-empowerment.

I'm able to tell when the energy in my throat center is blocked. My neck and throat feel restricted. My body holds the memories of not being able to make a sound, to speak my truth, to ask for what I need, and to set boundaries. The unexpressed energy from my pre- and perinatal experiences, bullying, work traumas, and other situations I've shared remains trapped. Once it comes into my awareness, I release the energy that has been stuck in my body. I've screamed to release energy related to the trauma of sexual abuse and other situations where I wanted to rage. I've personally used a whistle to blow out blocked energy. I have several clients who also use a whistle to clear their neck and throat. I sang the "Hannah My Delta Gamma" song in front of a group. Talking about how the song "others" and ridicules was one way of speaking my truth.

I'm aware that I can be loud and talk too much. These are signs of being in shock and they can also indicate that my throat chakra is holding too much energy. This is a clue to check in with my communication, expression, and truth-telling. I grind my teeth and sometimes experience neck stiffness and shoulder tension. Using the chakra system as my GPS, I simply become mindful and check in with my body. I then discern if my physical symptoms are letting me know my chakra is out of balance.

Practices I use to balance my throat chakra include energy release work (like the whistle and the Damn It Doll), painting, Reiki, and hypnotherapy.

Third-Eye Chakra. Light.
Past, Future, Imagination, Intuition, Expanded Possibilities

The third-eye chakra relates to inner vision, to perceiving truths that can't be detected with the eyes alone. Vivid dreams, clear thinking, wisdom, and out-of-body experiences emanate from this chakra.

In balance: enhances intuition and clarity of thought.

Out of balance: can cause confusion and lack of focus.

Excessive: delusions, hallucinations.

Deficient: cynical, close-mindedness, denial. Somatic experiences may include headaches, sinus problems, blurred vision, or eye sensitivity.

Offers the experience of integration, combining spiritual knowledge and experiences into daily life, leading to greater harmony and inner knowing.

It's clear that I was in denial (illusion), and confusion throughout the relationship with my manfriend and our plans to open a bed and breakfast, leaving my third eye energy center out of balance. Although I don't remember them, I believe that as an infant, I had out-of-body experiences while in the incubator as an attempt to escape feelings of earthly abandonment and to reconnect with God. Mystery school, metaphysical studies, meditation, breathwork, and decades-long participation in two spiritual mastermind groups have enhanced my intuition, integration of my physical body and spiritual body, and connection to Source.

Some practices I use to balance my third eye include meditation, water aerobics, using essential oils, breathwork, and chanting.

Crown Chakra
Spirituality, Unity, Enlightenment

The crown chakra relates to thought, higher mental powers, the generation of ideas, and our intellectual capacity.

In balance: brings a sense of unity and bliss.

Out of balance: may cause spiritual disconnection,

Excessive: disconnection from earthly reality, spiritual addiction, overly intellectual.

Deficient: disconnection from Spirit, cynical, close-minded. Somatic experiences may include dizziness, brain fog, poor sleep, and light sensitivity.

Offers a deep sense of connection to the divine or higher power, feelings of inner peace, and a heightened sense of purpose and meaning to life.

This chakra offers the opportunity to use one's spiritual insights and abilities to contribute to the greater good, fostering positive change in the world. Writing this book has been an incredible spiritual endeavor. Ideas flowed easily, helpful people have crossed my path, and my thinking has been clear. I felt very connected to God and grounded in the process. My purpose is evident, and my life is meaningful. Amid chaos in the world around me, I have increasing awareness of unity beyond family, community, and country. This quote, attributed to Desmond Tutu, resonates: "My humanity is bound up in yours, for we can only be human together."

As I continue to heal and progress on my path toward wholeness, practices such as meditation, contemplation, mindfulness, connections with my spiritual communities, and gratitude have become more automatic and authentic. I swim regularly, practice intuitive eating, try new recipes, connect with others on similar healing paths, monitor my progress (highlighting non-scale victories), trust my inner knowing, and let go of control.

This chakra-based framework can provide a structured yet flexible approach to personal and spiritual development. As described briefly, each chakra's state can affect physical, emotional, and spiritual well-being, serving as a map or GPS to spiritual and healing paths.

I've been reflecting, integrating, and gaining deeper understanding of the impact of imbalanced energy centers on my efforts to understand and heal my struggles with food and fear of hunger. Eating disorders can be linked to imbalances in multiple chakras, but I've listed those most closely associated:

Root Chakra: This chakra is related to our sense of security and grounding. When it's out of balance, it can lead to feelings of insecurity and instability, which may contribute to disordered eating behaviors.

Sacral Chakra: This chakra governs our emotions and creativity. An imbalance here can result in emotional instability and issues with self-worth, which are often seen in individuals with eating disorders.

Solar Plexus Chakra: This chakra is associated with personal power and self-esteem. When it's unbalanced, it can lead to low self-esteem and a lack of control, which are common in eating disorders.

I began my adventure with three essential questions in mind. First, I asked *what spiritual lessons am I to learn from my compulsive behaviors around food, hunger, eating, and body image?*

Over time, I've come to understand that when we are in illusion, we believe in the reality of the material world. This faulty belief obscures the ultimate truth of unity and the divine. The body is temporary, and the soul is eternal. Illusion leads people to identify with their physical bodies and material possessions. Illusion results in desires and attachments that distract from the pursuit of truth and self-realization. Illusion reinforces the idea that I am separate from God.

Part of my spiritual journey involves becoming aware of my attachments to the material world—to food, clothes, pretty things, happy feelings, looking good, to coffee, feeling accomplished, and to DO-ing things. I feel a deep sense of anxiety, loss, emptiness, and disconnection when my attachment to the physical world overrides my deep desire to feel and live in unity with the divine.

I'm learning that the ultimate goal is to manifest my spirituality into my body. I'm getting clarity about what it means to bring spirit into matter within my form. To be grounded (a word I've frequently used and taught but now understand more deeply) is to truly experience balance; to be a spiritual being in a physical body in a material world.

My body is important, precious, and perfect. Getting to know, love, have compassion for, and care for my physical being enhances my sense of purpose, good health, vitality, financial affluence, and joyful sensuality. In this physical world, I choose to treat my body as a vehicle for expressing love for myself and others.

What began as the physical hunger and needs that all infants have is really my spiritual hunger, a longing that food alone will not satisfy. I know in my soul that I am a multidimensional, divine, spiritual BE-ing.

My second question was *how do I heal so I can live my life fully, authentically, and peacefully?*

As a long-time in-and-out member of Weight Watchers, I've contemplated and shared my *why* many times. Why do I want to get healthy, lose weight and develop new habits now, and so on? For years, my *why* was some variation of this: I move with confidence, ease, and grace in my lean, healthy body at my daughter's wedding (class reunion, playing with grandkids, going on a date, making a TedTalk) wearing cool, colorful, flowing, clothes, and awesome jewelry.

I shared my current *why* earlier and will repeat it here:

The quest to blossom came from the depths of my soul. The tension between my insides (knowing that I am divine and perfect as is) and my outsides (eating-related behaviors that manifested as disturbances to living my whole, authentic life) became unbearable.

My compelling new *why* prompted me to walk both the spiritual and healing paths, and has significantly impacted how I am healing. I'm now able to offer the following to the world.

I trust my inner knowing and lovingly share how I am making peace with food and hunger. Today. Day-by-day.

I know that my obsessions/compulsions related to food, hunger, and body image are not my fault. They are trauma responses. I honor my hunger. It seems so simple. My consistent, conscious decision to eat when I am hungry, without rigid rules, and with no shame, is by far the most significant behavioral change I've made along my journey. I no longer fear eating without a plan. One day, I simply let go of trying to control food. I enjoy eating and cooking.

I've identified my emotional eating habits and if I overeat (we all do at times), I practice responding with compassion. Then I forget about it and go on with my awesome life. I regulate my nervous system and use tools to develop and strengthen heart coherence. I focus more on what I feel than what to eat. I've stopped the diet riot in my head.

I've accepted that part of my journey involves being patient. I'm no longer tantalized by quick fixes. This is a walk down the road that is less traveled. I identify stress triggers and stressful emotions. This involves mindfulness. I recognize and reduce emotional stress. I'm making an exciting shift from emotional eating to intuitive eating. I've tamed my inner critic. I'm releasing my need to control, all-or-nothing thinking, and perfectionism.

I trust my body. She knows when to breathe, how to swallow, how to keep my heart beating. I surrender to her wisdom. I know what I/we truly need. Love. Attention and Acceptance. Creative Expression. Spiritual Connection. Everyone's heart is their GPS as they make their hero's journey and ultimately make peace with food and hunger.

My final question was *what am I to create that will help others heal and raise their consciousness?*

My story ends where it started. "By offering up their life stories for scrutiny, these women were hoping to find some clues, some answers, to the origin of this mysterious obsession (with food, dieting, body image) that consumed their lives." -Anita Johnston

I AM these Women
My Gift is My Story

Writing and sharing my story is the medicine, the reward, the lost treasure now held in my heart, because I had the courage and support to venture out on my heroine's journey.

And now, I return with the elixir:

**"What I really want is love.
What I crave is attention and acceptance.
What I long for is creative expression.
What I yearn for is spiritual connection."**
December 2024

-With gratitude to Anita Johnston, *Eating in the Light of the Moon*
(p.39)

Journal Entry 12/8/23
I fell in love with myself today. This was not an intellectual 'I love myself.' This was a heart-cracked-open initiation by fire, rising from the Phoenix, limiting beliefs burned away moment.
I felt this love through my entire BE-ing! I sobbed. I grounded myself in this feeling by walking barefoot on the grass outside. My life changed today.

Personal acrylic painting: Armored Heart

"The courage it takes to share your story might be the very thing someone else needs to open their heart to hope."
-Unknown

"Other people are going to find healing in your wounds. Your greatest life messages and your most effective ministry will come out of your deepest hurts."
-Rick Warren

NOTES

1. Michael Mirdad. *The Seven Initiations on the Spiritual Path: Understanding the Purpose of Life's Tests.* (Bellingham, WA: Grail Press, 2011)
2. Mirdad. *The Seven Initiations on the Spiritual Path.*
3. Institute of HeartMath™. *Resilience Advantage™ Guidebook.*
4. Institute of HeartMath™. *Resilience Advantage™ Guidebook.*

THANKS FOR ACCOMPANYING ME ON MY HEROINE'S JOURNEY

"You are not a drop in the ocean, you are the entire ocean in a drop."
-Rumi

Like many others across time, cultures, and geography, we come into this world with a purpose. Our passion is driven by our innate motivation to grow spiritually, to increase our consciousness, and, in short, to remember who we truly are. We are each a magnificent manifestation of God, Spirit, Source, Nature, or whatever one calls the glorious energy that gave birth to the universe in the first place. It is said that we each have a spiritual committee in the heavenly realms. These beings assist us in developing our earthly plan. We choose our parents and siblings, where we'll "land," the circumstances of our birth and development, the people we'll meet, the whole shebang. Fortunately, when we reach a certain level of awareness, we recognize that our experiences, current events, our lives have been orchestrated so that we'll develop spiritually. We are energy, made of the elements that created the stars and the universe. We'll raise our vibration and hold greater light as we remember that God, Source, Spirit dwells in each of us.

This book has been a labor of love. The process of writing has also brought up new shadow parts to heal and integrate. I'm aware that impostor syndrome has been like an anchor weighing me down, and at times, my writing has stopped altogether for months and even for a year or two.

Impostor syndrome is a psychological pattern where individuals doubt their accomplishments and have a persistent fear of being exposed as a fraud, despite evident success. When I was able to step out of illusion, I recognized that my inner critic was screaming, "But you haven't figured this whole thing out! You are still overweight! You have to be perfect to be credible! You don't even know what elixir you're going to bring back! You don't know how the story is going to end!" Perfectionism is a common sign of impostor syndrome. Setting excessively lofty standards for myself and feeling disappointed when they're not met is a shadow part. I'm learning how to have more compassion for myself. My desire to share my story is far greater than the voice of the little critic. She now takes up far less space in my head!

I am a work in progress. As part of my training and practice, I still do hypnotherapy, psychodrama, and breathwork as a client and as a coach. I recently joined an incredible group of women who meet weekly to support each other in making peace with food, befriending our hunger, experiencing liberation from suffering, and seeing our light reflected in each other. Our facilitator understood that to heal, she needed to stop dieting. She's supported thousands of people on their healing journeys.

I can tell you that as I've stopped dieting, I've begun to make peace with food and my hunger. I have a small dove tattoo on my left wrist. She reminds me of the liberation I feel every day when I remember that I'm a divine soul in a physical body. And so are you.

It's not my intention that you'll become healed, whole, and healthy after reading my book. It's my hope that my story helps you to give voice to your story, and that your story facilitates understanding, compassion, and grace that helps you heal all levels of your BE-ing.

"When I dare to be powerful, to use my strength in the service of my vision, then it becomes less and less important whether I am afraid."
- Audre Lorde

ACKNOWLEDGMENTS

To my family, with love:
Jen, Ali, Quinn, Beau, Dexter, Carter, Jeff, and Tyler

For Yvonne, my teacher:
When I look in the mirror, I see the face of God.

With deep gratitude to my spiritual and wellness communities:
Amazing Grace, Fourth Borne, AOM

To my Master Mind groups:
Karen, Glo, Aida, and Dar
Des, Linda, Joey, Kendra

In awe and appreciation of the incredible healers in my life:
JZ, David, Dr. Mike, Rose, Tom, Michael, Carol, Charles, Janice,
Kimberly, Judy, Linda

Hugs to my siblings. You inspire me:
Ed, Jennie, Frank

With love to my parents who helped me to become the woman that I
am today:
Marjorie Eynon Purnell and Edward W. Purnell

With gratitude and compassion for my partners in marriage:
Bill and Ron

To those who have been like family to me, forever in my heart:
Nancy, Marc, Steve, Sally, Lee, Lynne, Sarah, Carolyn, Kate, Casey,
Catherine, Regina, Viviana

With gratitude to my fabulous editor:
Cindy Conger

ABOUT THE AUTHOR

Laura Purnell is a mom, grandmother, friend, teacher, coach, healer, and spiritual BE-ing. She's committed to helping raise human consciousness and is willing to be vulnerable in the process. This is the debut of Laura's first book.

While managing the ongoing "diet riot in her head," Laura began integrating her experiences as an urban school superintendent focused on educational equity, with her experiences and training in: Advanced Clinical Hypnotherapy (ACHT), Comprehensive Energy Psychology, Integral Breath Therapy, and treating trauma. She offers experiential training programs and transformational coaching focused on leadership, equity, wellbeing, and consciousness. In addition, she uses a variety of healing practices with individuals seeking physical, mental, emotional, and spiritual coherence.

Laura lives and leads from both her head and heart. She earned her doctorate in urban education, focusing on learning and development across the lifespan. She received her Advanced Clinical Hypnotherapy Certification from The Wellness Institute. She is a certified HeartMath™ Resilience Advantage Trainer™ and uses the Institute of HeartMath™ tools and technologies personally, and in her teaching, consulting, coaching, and healing.

In addition to her work as the Educational Alchemist, Laura has served as an Academic Superintendent, Turnaround School Superintendent, Assistant Superintendent, Deputy Chief of Leadership & Growth, and Principal. She and her turnaround principal teams studied at the prestigious Darden School of Business at the University of Virginia, where she earned her certification as a turnaround specialist. She was Co-Founder of Citizens' Academy, a nationally recognized community school in Cleveland, Ohio. Laura is passionate about cultural competence and diversity and has presented locally and nationally on this topic for more than thirty years.

Laura's hope is that her story will resonate with others who are tired of carrying the weight of a "diet riot" in their heads. A teacher at heart, she is launching a virtual course called Stop the Diet Riot!™ Laura's purpose is to stimulate curiosity and compassion among students as they explore and heal their baffling obsession with food, dieting, and body image. She envisions many heroes returning home from their journeys transformed, with newfound wisdom and authenticity, having made peace with food and hunger.

Educational Alchemist, LLC
www.educationalalchemist.com

laura@educationalalchemist.com

www.ingramcontent.com/pod-product-compliance
Lightning Source LLC
Chambersburg PA
CBHW051523120626
46551CB00012B/1057